I TOLD
YOU I
WAS ILL

> 'It's not that I'm afraid to die. I just don't want to be there when it happens.'
>
> WOODY ALLEN, WRITER AND DIRECTOR

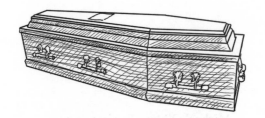

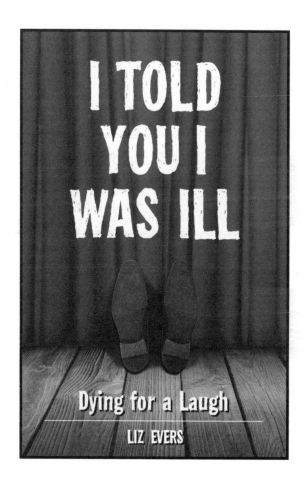

I TOLD YOU I WAS ILL

Dying for a Laugh

LIZ EVERS

Michael O'Mara Books Limited

First published in Great Britain in 2012 by
Michael O'Mara Books Limited
9 Lion Yard
Tremadoc Road
London SW4 7NQ

A CIP catalogue record for this book is available from the British Library.
Papers used by Michael O'Mara Books Limited are natural, recyclable
products made from wood grown in sustainable forests. The
manufacturing processes conform to the environmental regulations of
the country of origin.

ISBN: 978-1-84317-622-0 in hardback print format
ISBN: 978-1-84317-927-6 in EPub format
ISBN: 978-1-84317-928-3 in Mobipocket format

1 2 3 4 5 6 7 8 9 10

Cover design by Greg Stevenson
Designed and typeset by K.DESIGN, Winscombe, Somerset
Illustrations by Andrew Pinder

Printed and bound in Great Britain by Clays Ltd, St Ives plc

www.mombooks.com

CONTENTS

INTRODUCTION

RIP

Death may be grim and inevitable, but sometimes it's comedy gold. For your macabre pleasure, this compendium brings together some of the most hilarious headstone epitaphs ever chiselled, a range of spectacularly strange sendoffs and a litany of bizarre last requests performed in the name of all that is ridiculous.

You'll also find accounts of some of the most stylish exits in history: inventors done in by their own inventions, performers expiring on stage (more common than you'd think) and others that give a whole new meaning to the expressions 'dying for the loo' or 'to die laughing'.

The book brings together a host of wacky tales of faked deaths – the audacity and often sheer stupidity of which beggar belief – from the wealthy eccentric who staged his own funeral just to witness the grief he inspired, to the bumbling fraudster who forged his death certificate to avoid paying a minor speeding fine. There's also a rollcall of mistaken deaths and bungled obituaries including the one that led to the still-living US vice president Dick Cheney being eulogized as the 'UK's Favorite Grandmother'.

You can get the gossip on the top-ten earning deceased celebrities, the best place to be buried, and you'll even find some useful tips on planning your big day – from choosing the most ostentatious, attention-grabbing exit to selecting just the right music to accompany you on your final journey. And if death doesn't suit you, you'll find a handy guide to 'undeath' on page 183.

Throughout you'll come across last words from the great and good, and amusing musings on the end from comedians, writers and famous figures, as well as a miscellany of fabulous funereal facts.

GOING OUT IN STYLE

Spectacular, Profound and Plain Silly Expirations

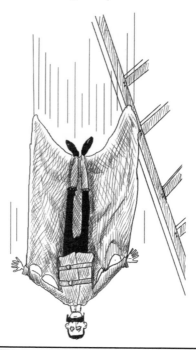

HOIST BY HIS OWN PETARD

You'd be surprised at just how many inventors are killed by their own inventions. One of the most famous examples is the unfortunate Austrian tailor Franz Reichelt, whose determination to create a parachute coat in which he could fly had inevitably tragic results.

In February 1912, Reichelt went to Paris to test his contraption from the top of the Eiffel Tower, telling the authorities he would use a dummy. This wasn't wholly untrue: he donned the coat himself and leapt from a sixty-metre deck to his death.

The grisly moment was even captured on film: forty-five seconds of footage of Reichelt preparing for his 'flight' and a four-second plunge. Those with hearty stomachs can view the British Pathé footage online.

Others who have fallen prey to their own creations include:

WILLIAM NELSON (1879–1903), a General Electric employee who invented an early motorized bicycle. He fell off his prototype during a test run.

THOMAS ANDREWS (1873–1912), lead shipbuilder of the Titanic who died on her maiden voyage.

MARIE CURIE (1867–1934) invented the process to isolate radium after co-discovering the radioactive elements radium and polonium. She died of prolonged exposure to radiation emanating from her research materials.

ALEXANDER BOGDANOV (1873–1928), pioneer of the blood transfusion. He gave himself eleven blood transfusions and died on the twelfth try.

JIMI HESELDEN (1948–2010), the British multi-millionaire entrepreneur and owner of the Segway company who died aged sixty-two. He was testing an all-terrain Segway when he lost control and drove the machine off a cliff.

The poet and grammarian **PHILETAS OF COS**, reputed to have died of insomnia in 270 BC. He was driven into deranged self-neglect trying to solve the liar paradox: 'I am lying now. This statement is false.'

JAMES DOUGLAS, the Earl of Morton (1516–81), who was executed in Scotland for his role in the murder of Henry Stuart, husband of Mary, Queen of Scots. The device used to kill him was known as 'The Maiden' – a nasty, guillotine-like contraption of his own making.

American fitness enthusiast **JIM FIXX** (1932–84), who while he couldn't be said to have 'invented' jogging, certainly popularized the activity through his bestselling book *The Complete Book of Running* in the 1970s. And yes, he died while jogging.

THOMAS MIDGLEY JR (1889–1944), the inventor and chemist who discovered CFCs died when he became tangled in the pulley system he invented for his mechanical bed, accidentally strangling himself.

'I want to die like my father: peacefully in his sleep. Not screaming and terrified like his passengers.'

BOB MONKHOUSE, COMEDIAN

THE SHOW MUST GO ON

Dying on stage is the ultimate dramatic exit. But to die on stage to peels of laughter when your audience thinks it is part of the act is a unique kind of comedy genius.

In 1673 the renowned French actor and comic playwright Molière died on stage after being seized by a violent coughing fit, much to his spectators' delight. He was playing the title role in his own play *Le Malade Imaginaire* (*The Hypochondriac*) – so you can see why the audience might be confused.

British slapstick comedian Tommy Cooper expired onstage of a heart attack in 1984 while performing at Her Majesty's Theatre in London and being broadcast live on national television. The audience tittered away as he lay on the floor, convinced the madcap performer was trying out some macabre new material.

In a cruel twist of fate, comedian Eric Morecambe died when he suffered a heart attack during a curtain call of his performance at a theatre in Tewkesbury, Gloucestershire. During the performance, he'd said he would hate to die like Tommy Cooper. Oh dear.

Corpulent opera singer Leonard Warren met a similar fate onstage at the New York Metropolitan Opera in 1960. Just as he launched into a section which translates as 'to die, a momentous thing', he was seized by a coughing fit and fell to the ground, dying of a massive heart attack. Momentous indeed.

A street rather than a stage performance was the last for fifty-three-year-old morris dancer Peter Hardy. During a performance in 2005 in Newmarket, England, Hardy's heart gave out mid-dance. One wonders whether some people in the audience were secretly relieved that the bizarre traditional dance was brought to an early end.

American comedy actor and stand-up Dick Shawn (1924–87) died onstage during a rather fitting skit. Shawn was poking fun at the campaign cliché of politicians, 'I will not lay down on the job!', and to demonstrate laid face down on the floor. Naturally the audience thought that it was all part of the show, until a theatre employee began administering CPR, followed soon after by the paramedics.

Famous Last Words

'It was the food. It was the food.'

ACTOR RICHARD HARRIS (1930–2002) to diners as he was carried by stretcher through the lobby of London's swanky Savoy Hotel for his final journey to hospital.

YOU'RE KILLING ME!

If you've got to go there are worse ways than to die laughing. Such was the case for fifty-year-old Kings Lynn brickie Alex Mitchell who laughed so hard at a classic episode of British comedy, *The Goodies*, that he suffered a heart attack. The cheerful epilogue to that story is that Mitchell's wife Nessie, wrote to the programme makers to thank them for making her husband's last half hour so happy.

In a similar incident, two centuries before, a Mrs Fitzherbert was thoroughly tickled by the vision of a man dressed as a woman onstage at London's Drury Lane theatre.

So much so that she began to laugh so raucously that she could not desist and had to leave the theatre but was unable to banish the image from her head. Each time she thought of it the laughter would return more hysterically than before – until she reached fever pitch, was overcome with hilarity, and died.

A particularly hilarious pub joke led to the demise of poet and critic Lionel Johnson in 1902 – he fell from his bar stool because of the force of his laughter, fatally cracking his skull on the floor. Just what the joke was, we'll never know.

In the seventeenth century, the usually dour Scottish aristocrat and polymath Thomas Urquhart died during a fit of laughter brought on by the news that Charles II had retaken the throne of England.

One of the first recorded instances of death by laughter is that of Zeuxis of Heraclea, a Greek artist, who in the fifth century BC died of a burst blood vessel caused by uncontrollably cackling at his own painting of an old woman who had paid him to portray her as Aphrodite, goddess of love.

Another ancient who died by hilarity was Chrysippus of Soli, 280–207 BC, a founder of the Stoic school of philosophy. He cracked up and keeled over after giving his donkey wine and watching the drunken animal attempt to eat figs.

DYING FOR A WEE. LITERALLY

In 2006, twenty-eight-year-old Jennifer Lea Strange from Rancho Cordova, California, met an end worthy of her surname. The young mother of three was found dead in her home hours after trying to win a Nintendo Wii games console on air on the KDND 107.9 radio station. The ill-advised game she was playing? 'Hold Your Wee for a Wii', a contest which involved drinking large quantities of water without urinating. Strange died of 'hyperhydration', also known as water intoxication.

In Belgium in 2005, an unfortunate woman got caught short on her way home from a bar one night. The twenty-nine-year-old took a shortcut through a cemetery, selected a discreet spot to relieve herself but mid-flow one of the headstones above her toppled and crushed her to death.

Renowned seventeenth-century Danish astronomer Tycho Brahe met his inglorious end at a royal banquet when, fearing bad manners, he stayed at the table rather than answer the pressing call of nature and ruptured his bladder.

South African Detective Sergeant Daniel Edwards was found crushed to death between his car and a tree in 1997 after apparently getting out for a wee, leaving his car on an incline above him without the handbrake on.

Miami construction worker Ramon Jose Rodriguez's perfect safety record came to an abrupt end on a building site in 1998, when a portable toilet on top of a four-storey building was blown on top of him by high winds.

In 2008 at Vauxhall train station, London, a Polish tourist met with a rather unfortunate end when he urinated onto a live rail surging with 750 volts and electrocuted himself. The entire incident was recorded for posterity on CCTV.

NEVER WORK WITH CHILDREN OR ANIMALS OR FLIES...

Sadly this advice came too late for diminutive Austrian acrobat Franz Dasch in 1999. In a spectacular – if unplanned – last stunt Dasch trampolined straight into the wide-open mouth of a nearby hippo that was yawning at the time and swallowed him whole. The 7,000 or so spectators watching the act in north Thailand assumed this incredible feat was part of a grand finale and cheered uproariously.

Another large animal-related fatality befell zookeeper Friedrich Reisfeldt while he was treating his charge, an elephant called Stefan for constipation. Having fed the huge beast a combination of laxatives and prunes, Reisfeldt was unfortunately positioned behind Stefan as his ministrations took effect. He suffocated to death beneath ninety kilos of elephant poo.

Considerably smaller animals were involved – albeit as intended victims – when in 2007 a sixty-three-year-old German man resolved to rid his garden of moles once and for all. Planning to run enough high-voltage energy into his vegetable patch to operate a cement mixer, he electrocuted himself the moment he flipped the switch. Not a single mole was harmed in his fatal experiment.

Smaller yet was the creature that, in 1159, did in Pope Adrian IV (the only Englishman ever to reach the highest, holiest office). While delivering a withering speech in Rome, excommunicating the reigning Emperor Frederick I, a fly flew into his mouth, causing him to choke to death.

Famous Last Words

'One of us must go.'

OSCAR WILDE'S (1854–1900) last comments on the dreadful decor in the room in which he lay dying. This quote is sometimes extended to: 'Either this wallpaper goes or I do.' He's also credited with the last words, 'I am dying as I have lived: beyond my means' while quaffing a final glass of champagne.

DEAD DRUNK

Alcohol kills a lot of people every year – some more stylishly than others. Take Joan Scovell of Connecticut who, one early morning in 1985, attempted to climb onto Freda, a rather ample circus elephant, weighing in at 2,950 kilos. Sadly Joan was alone in thinking this was a hilarious prank, as Freda grabbed Joan with her trunk and threw her to the ground, and her death.

Though it sank some hundred years ago, the *Titanic* still has a deadly power, as the rather intoxicated Emma Blackwell from Plymouth, England, learned on a cross-channel ferry. Striking an open-armed Kate Winslet pose to the sea at the front of the boat, poor Emma lost her footing and fell nine decks down into the water below.

Bringing a whole new meaning to the expression 'pissed as a newt', a drunken daredevil died after swallowing a newt on a prank. It turned out to be a rough-skinned newt, capable of producing a toxin deadly to humans.

Booze performed a pre-emptive strike on Clifton Doan of Idaho in 1992. When he opened his fridge door for a beer the cracked keg inside shot upwards, into his face, killing him instantly.

None other than Attila the Hun was an early victim of the demon drink. He expired on his wedding night in AD 453, when he drunkenly drowned in his own blood from a nosebleed.

GOING OUT
WITH A BANG

Being the widow of a world-renowned aeronaut, a man who fearlessly demonstrated the first parachute, one might have assumed that Madame Blanchard would know a thing or two about air travel, but apparently not. She definitely knew a thing or two about putting on a crowd-pleasing show, however. And so it was that in 1819 Madame Blanchard sought to extravagantly mark her ascent over Paris in a hot air balloon by letting off fireworks. As onlookers gazed up at her the celebratory display quickly went horribly wrong when the balloon caught fire and Madame Blanchard plunged to her death from a great height.

At a quaint English village fête in 1979 an unfortunate vicar volunteered to sit atop a tank of water while paying punters threw balls at him in an attempt to knock him in. His inevitable dunking was not quite as hilarious as it might have been – given the vicar was holding a live microphone when he plunged into the water.

More recently in 2011 in Kent, England, a gentleman's first job as a human cannonball went horribly wrong. It was all going so well – he was shot from the cannon and flew elegantly through the air towards the net ... or at least to where the net should have been. According to witnesses at the scene it collapsed just as the man hurtled towards it from a height of some thirty feet. He crashed head first into the ground at speed, in front of a crowd of 2,000 horrified people.

It was the clatter of coffins that killed undertaker Marc Bourjade in 1982. He was crushed under a pile of them in his workshop. Fittingly he was buried in one of the offending articles.

> 'I read *The Times* and if my name is not in the obits I proceed to enjoy the day.'
>
> NOEL COWARD, WRITER AND WIT

ATTEMPTED MURDER, MURDER AND SUICIDE IN ONE FELL SWOOP

Probably one of the most famous and bizarre accidental death stories doing the rounds is that of Ronald Opus who took his own life (sort of) in 1994. When a despairing Opus threw himself from a tenth-storey window he forgot that a recently installed safety net, placed there to protect workers renovating the building, would break his fall just a couple of floors down.

However, by bizarre coincidence, he fell past the ninth floor just as an elderly gent was threatening his wife with a shotgun, which was accidentally discharged – shooting the falling Opus as he descended.

Not only that, but the elderly gent revealed that it was his habit to threaten his wife with the shotgun when they argued, but that it had never been loaded. That is until just a few weeks previous to the shooting when it was loaded without his knowledge by his son ... one Ronald Opus.

It turned out that Ronald had loaded the gun in the hope that his father would accidentally shoot his mother, who had cut him off financially, during one of their many arguments. However, when the hoped-for accident never happened, Ronald despaired and threw himself off their apartment building – only to be shot by the gun.

Ultimately the medical examiner on the case ruled that Ronald's death was suicide.

A LAST HURRAH!

If you've got to go, there are few better ways to expire than in the throes of passion (though other people present at the moment of death might dispute that). Here are some of the more unusual instances of people passing away with their pants down:

French President **FELIX FAURE** (1841–99) died of good old-fashioned 'apoplexy' while his thirty-year-old office assistant was performing a particularly intimate act upon him. So scared was she by the event that she reportedly got lockjaw and required significant assistance detaching herself from her lover's body.

Another politician, forty-first Vice President of the United States **NELSON ROCKEFELLER** (1908–79), is widely thought to have expired shortly after performing 'the act' with his younger aide. To cover up the truth of their affair, it is thought that his aide oversaw a *Weekend at Bernie's*-style farce in which Rockefeller was dressed, removed to his office and positioned so that it would appear as if he had had his heart attack at his desk. An ambulance wasn't called until an hour after his heart attack, by which time it was too late to save him.

British MP **STEPHEN MILLIGAN** (have you spotted a trend yet?) breathed his last while engaging in some seemingly solo fun. The Conservative politician was found dead in his London home 'naked except for a pair of stockings and suspenders' according to police. His death was not treated as suspicious and it further emerged that he was found with a black bin liner on his head – indicating he died as a consequence of so-called 'auto-erotic asphyxiation'. The coroner ruled 'death by misadventure'. Others who have mis-adventured thus include actor David Carradine and INXS singer Michael Hutchence who both accidentally hung themselves in pursuit of pleasure.

Famous Last Words

'Pardon me, sir. I did not do it on purpose.'

QUEEN MARIE 'Let them eat cake' Antoinette's (1755–93) apologetic last words after she accidentally stepped on the foot of her executioner as she went to the guillotine. Bit late for apologies some might say.

A MISCELLANY OF FUNNY FATALITIES...

Some final moments just can't be categorized. Below you'll find some strange and usual deaths that are truly, tragically unique.

Death by beard

In the sixteenth century, Austrian Hans Steininger was renowned throughout Europe for his prodigious beard, presumed to be the longest in the world at an incredible 1.4 metres. But in the end Steininger paid quite a price for his hirsute celebrity – in 1567 he tripped over his beard while fleeing a burning tower, and plunged down the stairs to his death.

Death by orange peel

The insane practice of going over the powerful Niagara Falls in a barrel had its heyday in the early twentieth century and usually resulted in the death of those mad enough to have a go. Not so the brave but clearly barmy Bobby Leach who became the second man to survive the plunge in 1911. But poor Leach came to a rather inglorious end in New Zealand during a tour publicizing his watery exploits – he slipped on a piece of orange peel and died of his injuries.

Death by irritation

Tennessee's most famous distiller of whiskey, Jack Daniel, met his end as a consequence of a fit of irritation early one morning in 1911. Having come into work at an ungodly hour, Daniel found he'd forgotten the combination for his safe and duly kicked it in frustration, sustaining a nasty toe injury. His damaged toe became infected and killed him. The moral of the story is that starting work too early in the day is bad for your health.

Death by moon

Considered to be one of China's greatest ever poets Li Po (AD 701–762) was also one of its greatest drunks. Renowned for flights of poetic, romantic fancy when he'd had a few, one night Li Po fell from a boat and drowned in the Yangtze River while reportedly trying to embrace the reflection of the moon in the water.

Death by dessert

On the night of 12 February 1771 King Adolf Frederick of Sweden embarked on a remarkable meal consisting of lobster,

caviar, sauerkraut, kippers and champagne. Far from sated by this luxurious fare, the king topped it off with a truly gluttonous fourteen servings of his favourite dessert – 'semla', a traditional Scandinavian pastry. Perhaps not surprisingly the king suffered from digestive problems and expired later that night. It was certainly a memorable last meal by anyone's standard.

Death by re-creation

Clement Vallandigham was an Ohio politician-turned-successful lawyer who seldom lost in court. In 1871 he took on the case of Thomas McGehan, who was accused of shooting a man named Tom Myers during a barroom brawl. Vallandigham's innovative defence was that Myers had accidentally shot himself while drawing his pistol from a kneeling position.

Vallandigham decided to demonstrate this 'accident' for the jury. Unfortunately, he took hold of a loaded gun by mistake and ended up shooting himself. Vallandigham's subsequent death by self-inflicted gunshot wound demonstrated the plausibility of the accidental shooting and his client was acquitted.

Vallandigham wasn't the only person unfortunate enough to do himself in via re-creation. In 1991 a fifty-seven-year-old Thai woman named Yooket Paen was walking in her farm when she accidentally slipped in cow dung, grabbed a live wire and was electrocuted to death. Shortly after her funeral, Paen's younger sister was demonstrating to her neighbours how the accident happened when she herself slipped, grabbed the same live wire and was also electrocuted to death.

Death by baseball

Back in 1920 Cleveland Indians player Ray Chapman became the first man to be killed by a baseball pitch. It was then common practice for pitchers to dirty the ball to make it harder for the hitter to see. In this case the pitcher did such a good job that Chapman didn't spot the ball in time to duck and it caught him full in the head, killing him.

Death by scarf

Isadora Duncan (1877–1927) was renowned for her grace as a dancer and her fondness for flowing scarves. Sadly, the latter was to be her undoing. Isadora died in a tragically bizarre motor accident in Nice, France, when her silk scarf became caught in the open-spoked wheels of the Bugatti car she was travelling in and broke her neck.

Upon her death the writer Gertrude Stein remarked that 'affectations can be dangerous'.

Death by hoarding

Note: filling your house with hoarded junk and setting booby traps to protect it is never a good idea. So discovered compulsive hoarders Homer and Langley Collyer, who meticulously kept everything they ever spent money on, from newspapers to furniture. They filled the rooms of their shared house from floor to ceiling with crap, setting traps to ward off potential thieves of their 'precious' booty.

And so one day in 1947, the police received an anonymous tip-off that there was a dead body at the Collyer house. When they finally managed to gain entrance through the blockade of rubbish, they found the body of Homer but there was no sign of his brother Langley. It took two more weeks for the police to wade through and remove some one hundred tons of detritus before uncovering the decomposing corpse of Langley – just a few feet from where his brother had lain.

The police concluded that Langley had been crawling through a tunnel under the piles of accumulated rubbish to bring his paralysed brother some food when he set off one of his own booby traps and was crushed under the weight of the falling tunnel 'walls'. Poor Homer must have starved to death waiting for the meal that never came.

Famous Last Words

'I am about to – or I am going to – die: either expression is correct.'

DOMINIQUE BOUHOURS (1628–1702), French Jesuit priest, grammarian and pedant to the very end.

Death by bragging

Healthy eating advocate and pioneer of organic farming Jerome Irving Rodale expired while being interviewed by American TV presenter Dick Cavett in 1971. Having bragged that he would 'live to a hundred, unless I'm run down by a sugar-crazy taxi driver', Rodale died of a heart attack mid-interview. Appearing fast asleep, Dick Cavett joked, 'Are we boring you, Mr Rodale?' before discovering that his seventy-two-year-old guest had in fact died. The show was never aired.

Death by rogue robot

The first man to fall foul of a robot was American Robert Williams in 1979. Williams climbed into a storage rack at a Ford motor plant to retrieve a part when the robot whose job it was had seemingly malfunctioned. However, the robot suddenly reactivated and slammed its arm into Williams's head, killing him instantly.

The second recorded death by robot occurred in 1981 when thirty-seven-year-old Japanese maintenance engineer Kenji Urada was working on a broken robot at a Kawasaki plant. Urada had failed to turn it off properly and the robot's mechanical arm accidentally pushed him into a grinding machine.

Death by avenging cactus

Many a lumberjack has been killed by a falling tree, but twenty-seven-year-old American David Grundman is probably the only person with the dubious distinction of being done in by a cactus he felled.

In 1982 Grundman and his roommate decided to go 'cactus plugging', aka shooting desert plants with a shotgun. When he opened fire on a hundred-year-old, twenty-six-foot-tall Saguaro cactus, Grundman blasted off a chunk large enough to crush him to death – which it promptly did. Nature had its revenge, and Grundman's family had a rather embarrassing eulogy to deliver.

Death by belly

British pro wrestler Mal 'King Kong' Kirk died underneath the bloated belly of Shirley 'Big Daddy' Crabtree in August 1987.

As Big Daddy concluded the match with his trademark 'Belly-Splash' move – which involved jumping up and down, slamming his ample belly onto King Kong – his opponent had a heart attack and died.

Big Daddy was not held responsible for King Kong's demise as it was revealed that he was suffering from a serious heart condition prior to the match, but he nonetheless blamed himself and decided to retire from pro wrestling.

Before the match, King Kong had reportedly told his friends: 'If I have to go, I hope it is in the ring.'

Death by sheep ... and motorcycle

In 1999, sixty-seven-year-old Betty Stobbs of Durham in England was delivering a bale of hay by motorbike to her hungry flock of sheep. But so hungry were the sheep that the sight of the incoming meal led to a stampede, which ultimately ended in Betty being knocked her off her bike and falling some one hundred feet into a quarry. She is thought to have survived the fall only to be killed by her motorbike, which fell into the quarry after her.

> 'At my age, flowers scare me.'
>
> GEORGE BURNS, COMEDIAN

ANY LAST REQUESTS?

Weird Wills and Confounding Funerals

BOUND FOR IMMORTALITY

Work was everything to practical joker Mark Gruenwald, writer at Marvel Comics. So much so in fact that his last request was that his ashes be mixed with ink and used to print the paperback version of his magnum opus, *Squadron Supreme*.

There are some 4,000 copies of this rather unique book in existence but it's very rare to find anyone willing to part with theirs – largely through superstition.

Another comic book eccentric, Dave Cockrum, died in bed in 2006 wearing his Superman pyjamas and covered by a Batman blanket. He was cremated in his best Green Lantern shirt.

STAKE ME OUT

Perhaps under the influence of one too many Hammer Horror movies, in 1972 British doctor Harold West left instructions for his doctor to pound a steel stake through his heart so he wouldn't come back as a vampire.

One of the best-known Draculas, the Hungarian Bela Lugosi (1882–1956), had a healthier relationship with his beloved role – demanding that he be buried in his count's cape.

I'LL BE BACK

John Bowman left a $50,000 trust fund so that a team of staff could maintain his twenty-one-room mansion, and mausoleum, from his death in 1891 to when the money ran out. In addition to maintenance the servants had to prepare a family meal every night for Bowman and his dead relatives.

Why? Because Mr Bowman had been convinced that he and his family would be reincarnated together and would be hungry when they returned to the house in their new bodies. Nobody knows if they did come back. The cash dried up in 1950, as did the dinners.

> 'One dies only once, and it's for
> such a long time!'
> MOLIÈRE, PLAYWRIGHT

DEATH WISH

Audrey Jean Knauer loved Charles Bronson's movie *Death Wish*. So much so that she left its star a whopping $300,000 in her will, despite the fact that she'd never met him. Needless to remark, her family contested her handwritten will, in which she specified that her mother should get nothing.

But the oddest part of the story is the fact that Charles Bronson actually took a substantial portion of the money! Although he said it was destined for charity ...

Famous Last Words

'Damn it ... Don't you dare ask
God to help me.'

Arch-eyebrowed Hollywood screen icon
JOAN CRAWFORD (1905–77) to her housekeeper, who
had the audacity to pray aloud at her deathbed.

BOARD STIFF

Philosopher and social reformer Jeremy Bentham left his body to medical science and, as requested in his will, it was dissected as part of a public anatomy lecture. Afterwards, the skeleton and head were preserved and kept inside a wooden cabinet known as the 'Auto-icon'. The skeleton was stuffed with hay and dressed in Bentham's clothes and topped off with a wax head. This fetching Auto-icon was acquired and put on public display by University College London in 1850 and for the 100th and 150th anniversaries of the college it was brought to the meeting of the College Council, where it was listed as 'present but not voting'.

SECOND BEST BED

The world's most famous playwright, William Shakespeare (1564–1616), is often criticized for his seeming mistreatment of his wife Anne. He got her pregnant, married but then abandoned her for a life in the theatre in London and finally, adding insult to injury, left her only his 'second best bed' in his will, splitting the remainder up between his children and friends.

However, others like me prefer not to think so ill of the great Mr S. Anne probably automatically inherited a large portion of his estate hence this wouldn't need to be specified in the will. And diehard romantics even choose to see it as a knowing gift from husband to wife, as in all likelihood the second best bed was their marriage bed, the best bed being reserved for guests.

INFERNAL RACKET

'Mad as a hatter' is an all-too-appropriate expression for milliner S. Sanborn. When he passed away in 1871, he stipulated that his skin be stretched into a set of drums and given to a friend.

Not only did he bequeath this odd gift to his lucky friend but it came with a request: every year on 17 June, he was required to go to Bunker Hill and play 'Yankee Doodle' on his friend-skin drum.

THE LAST LAUGH

The American comedian W. C. Fields was such a secretive, and some might say paranoid, individual that he had 200 bank accounts round the world under fictitious names and he kept no records of any of them. His executors were only able to find forty-five of these bank accounts, but the remaining deposits – estimated at $600,000 – were never found.

Although he famously once said, 'Anybody who hates children and dogs can't be all bad,' Fields left instructions for a college for orphans to be founded 'where no religion of any sort is to be preached'. He also left his mistress $15,000 more than his wife, as well as two bottles of perfume and a Cadillac. And his dictionary.

NO WOMEN ADMITTED

In 1930, the last wish of Iowan lawyer T. M. Zink was that his $50,000 fortune be left in trust for seventy-five years. At the end of this time he hoped the fund would have swelled to $3 million, enough to found the 'Zink Womanless Library', where the words 'No Women Admitted' were to mark each entrance. No books, works of art, or decorations by women were to be permitted in the library either. Zink explained: 'My intense hatred of women is not of recent origin or development nor based upon any personal differences I ever had with them but is the result of my experiences with women, observations of them, and study of all literatures and philosophical works.' Zink's dream never came true, however, as his family, which, of course, included some female members, successfully contested the will.

'Death is just nature's way of telling
you to slow down.'
DICK SHARPLES, BRITISH SCREENWRITER

FLY ME TO
THE MOON

Astronomer Dr Eugene Shoemaker, co-discoverer of the catchy-titled Comet Shoemaker-Levy 9, had his ashes put on the space probe Lunar Prospector in 1997 and buried on the moon. He's the only person to be laid to rest there.

There are, however, some 250 or so people 'buried' in outer space through a special arrangement with NASA. They include *Star Trek* creator Gene Roddenberry and James Doohan who played 'Scotty' on the show, as well as hippy and LSD advocate Timothy Leary.

LOTTERY LEGACY

When writing his will, a generous Portuguese gentleman selected seventy random beneficiaries from the Lisbon phonebook. When he passed away over a decade later in 2007, each of his unwitting recipients received a tidy €8,500 each.

DRESSING DOWN

Author Charles Dickens requested that mourners 'who attend my funeral wear no scarf, cloak, black bow, long hatband, or other such revolting absurdity'. In addition to this, Dickens also stated that his funeral details were to be kept private, that it was to be a simple, inexpensive affair with only three plain 'mourning coaches'. His family had other ideas, however, and his funeral was in fact staged on a grand scale, with a massive cortège and everyone decked out in the very revolting absurdities that he had expressly written against. Far from being private – his funeral was a national event. We can only hope that secretly Charles would have been pleased ...

Famous Last Words

'Bugger Bognor.'

KING GEORGE V (1865–1936), upon being told he would
soon be well enough to revisit Bognor Regis where he had
previously convalesced in 1929.

DEMOCRACY AND DIAMONDS

'Founding Father' of America Benjamin Franklin's dying wish was that his daughter respect the democracy he'd helped establish by refraining from 'the expensive, vain and useless pastime of wearing jewels'.

The reason for this request was that during his time as American ambassador to France, Franklin was given a portrait of King Louis XVI in a frame studded with 408 diamonds, which he left to this same daughter Sarah. It is presumed this was to stop her pilfering the jewels to make adornments. It's not known whether she obeyed this last request.

WARDROBE WARNING

The multimillionaire, former Olympiad, John B. Kelly, expressed a final wish that the clothing bills of his daughter, Princess Grace (Kelly), not bankrupt the principality of Monaco.

This request was one of many in his will giving Kelly the last laugh at the expense of his family including leaving his son John 'all my personal belongings, such as trophies, rings, jewellery, watches, clothing and athletic equipment, except the ties, shirts, sweaters and socks, as it seems unnecessary to give him something of which he has already taken possession'. He also left nothing to his son-in-law, Prince Rainier of Monaco, stating:

> I don't want to give the impression that I am against sons-in-law. If they are the right type, they will provide for themselves and their families, and what I am able to give my daughters will help pay the dress-shop bills, which, if they continue as they started out, under the able tutelage of their mother, will be quite considerable.

TOPSY-TURVY

In 1800, a Briton of French lineage named Peter Labelliere was laid to rest with some wonderfully eccentric twists. He requested that his landlady's two youngest children dance on his coffin at the funeral, then that it be buried vertically on the top of Box Hill. This second request was apparently because Labelliere believed that the 'world is turned topsy-turvy' and that when Armageddon came, he would be the only one standing the right way up. His grave is now a favourite picnicking spot for Box Hill visitors.

FERRARI FUNERAL

In 1977, Sandra West, a fabulously wealthy eccentric, requested that she be buried in a lace nightgown . . . at the wheel of her beloved vintage Ferrari.

In order to bury her in this elaborate fashion, both the deceased and her car had to be loaded into a concrete container and lowered into the ground by crane. Glamorous.

ONCE YOU POP...

Back in the 1960s one Fredric Baur changed the world of crisps as we know it – with the invention of the Pringles tube. When he passed away in 2008, it was his last request that part of his cremated remains be interred in one of his trademark tubes. Whether it kept them a little fresher than the average urn we'll never know.

LEAVING MONEY TO THE LORD

In the late 1970s a man called Ernest Digweed left a generous $47,000 to Jesus on the condition that the Lord has one hundred years to show up and claim the money or it all goes to the state.

So far a number of cash-strapped 'saviours' have appeared to claim the money but, as yet, none have provided sufficient evidence of their godliness. But there's still plenty of time left for any legitimate Chosen Ones out there ...

47

'They say such nice things about people
at their funerals that it makes me sad that
I'm going to miss mine by just a few days.'

GARRISON KEILLOR, WRITER AND HUMORIST

OTHERWORLDLY UNDERWEAR

Back in 1929 Reverend John Gwyon left a very generous $50,000 with the instructions that it be used to buy underwear for 'worthy boys' of his small town. Furthermore each garment was to carry the label 'Gwyon's Present' stitched into the lining.

KEEPING IT IN THE FAMILY

Mrs Robert Hayes spent her last days on earth fretting about what would become of her current husband and her stepdaughter from a previous marriage upon her demise. So, she did what any diligent mother and wife wouldn't and requested that the two marry within a week of her funeral. So, a few short days after her death her thirty-five-year-old widowed husband and twenty-one-year-old stepdaughter actually tied the knot. Just a little bit icky.

Famous Last Words

'Tomorrow, I shall no longer be here.'

Proving his mystical powers at the very end, this prophetic dying utterance is attributed to that apocalyptic visionary NOSTRADAMUS (1503–66).

SOUL-SEARCHING

Miner and hermit James Kidd was declared dead in 1956, having disappeared in 1949. In 1963 his handwritten will was discovered, revealing that he wanted the majority of his $275,000 estate to be spent on a search for some scientific proof of a soul which leaves the human body at death.

In the years that followed, the courts of Arizona had to dismiss more than one hundred petitions for the money from self-appointed soul-searchers. In 1971 the money was finally split between the American Society for Psychical Research and the Psychical Research Foundation.

Sadly, neither has made a convincing case for the soul's existence … yet.

POETIC JUSTICE

In 1856 German poet Heinrich Heine left his estate to his wife with one condition – she must remarry, so that 'there will be at least one man to regret my death'.

NO MO

Upon his death in 1862 clean-shaven Henry Budd left a sizeable £200,000 trust fund for his two sons. But there was a catch – neither of them could ever grow a moustache.

SWEET REVENGE

Variously attributed to an anonymous Irishman and a wealthy New Yorker, the following final deed of defiance acts as a cautionary tale to complacent family members: 'To my wife, I leave her lover and the knowledge that I was not the fool she thought me. To my son, I leave the pleasure of earning a living. For twenty years he thought the pleasure was mine – he was mistaken.'

THE FINEST NOSE

A French doctor left a substantial sum of money to be used as an annual prize awarded to any man or woman possessing 'the finest nose'. The competition was open to all nationalities, except Russians. However, there was a catch – competitors had to have red hair and black eyebrows.

HEIR HAIR HERE

Napoleon Bonaparte (1769–1821) was known for a great many 'eccentricities', most of which had appalling consequences for those he ruled over. One last request of his sums up the innate peculiarity of the pint-sized despot: he asked that his head be shaved and the hair divided up among his friends.

An intriguing twist to the tale came years later, when an analysis of some of the hair kept by his friends was discovered to contain large amounts of arsenic. Coupled with what is known of his symptoms prior to death (vomiting blood), this discovery indicates that Napoleon was poisoned. The official verdict prior to this was death from stomach cancer.

> 'The report of my death was an exaggeration.'
> MARK TWAIN, NOVELIST

GREAT STORK DERBY OF 1926

Canadian practical joker Charles Vance Millar left a will littered with weird and wonderful requests upon his death in 1926, including leaving his vacation house in Jamaica in the joint custody of three people whom he knew hated each other. But the most famous clause stated that the cash value of his estate was to be given to the woman who gave birth to the most children within a ten-year period. And so began the 'Great Stork Derby' in which numerous women from Toronto competed for the generous prize. The Supreme Court tried to stop the madness, but Millar had ensured the clause was legally airtight. In the end four women split the title, taking home $125,000 each – a considerable sum that would come in very handy in the raising of their nine children apiece.

Famous Last Words

'Now, now, my good man, this is no time for making enemies.'

A wit till the last, the French writer VOLTAIRE (1694–1778) responds to a priest's request that he renounce Satan on his deathbed.

BLOOD SACRIFICE? NO THANKS

The acerbic, irreligious Irish playwright George Bernard Shaw (1856–1950) ordered that no religious service be conducted for his funeral and that his tombstone not 'take the form of a cross or any other instrument of torture or symbol of blood sacrifice'. Shaw also used his will to express his support for 'Darwin's millennial saga of creation' over the Bible's 'six-day synopsis'.

The English language was intended to be a major beneficiary of Shaw's will. In life, he had been interested in reforming English spelling and even created a forty-letter phonetic alphabet to make spelling much simpler. His will provided a large portion of his estate to promote this new alphabet. Unfortunately this last request could not be honoured as it was overruled by a court as 'impossible' to implement and so the money was distributed to the British Museum, the National Gallery of Ireland, and the Royal Academy of Dramatic Art.

I WOZ 'ERE

Hilarious Headstones

STARS OF STAGE AND SCREEN

Those in the business often relish one last opportunity to entertain.

'She did it the hard way.'

BETTE DAVIS (1908–89), Hollywood actress

'That's all folks.'

MEL BLANC (1908–89), voice of
Bugs Bunny, Porky Pig, Daffy Duck, and many more

'Life is a jest, and all things show it.
I thought so once, and now I know it.'

JOHN GAY (1685–1732), poet and playwright

'I told you I was ill.'

SPIKE MILLIGAN (1918–2002), comedian

Famous Last Words

'Don't let it end like this!
Tell them I said something!'

The last words of Mexican revolutionary PANCHO VILLA
(1878–1923) to a nearby journalist as he died of a bullet
wound sustained in battle.

DIDN'T MAKE THE GRAVE

These excellent epitaphs – suggested by the stars themselves – sadly all ended up on the cutting-room floor.

'Exit Burbage.'

RICHARD BURBAGE (1568–1619), Shakespearian actor

'I'm involved in a plot.'

Alfred Hitchcock (1899–1980), Director

'Excuse my dust.'

DOROTHY PARKER (1893–1967), Humorist

'Back to the silent.'

CLARK GABLE (1901–60), Hollywood actor

'On the whole I'd rather be in Philadelphia.'

W. C. FIELDS (1880–1946), Comedian

'Here lies Groucho Marx
And Lies and Lies and Lies
P.S. he never kissed an ugly girl.'

GROUCHO MARX (1890–1977), Comic actor

'The body of
B. Franklin, Printer
(Like the Cover of an Old Book
Its Contents torn Out
And Stript of its Lettering and Gilding)
Lies Here, Food for Worms.
But the Work shall not be Lost;
For it will (as he Believ'd) Appear once More
In a New and More Elegant Edition
Revised and Corrected
By the Author.'

BENJAMIN FRANKLIN (1706–90)

'Posterity will ne'er survey
A nobler grave than this.
Here lie the bones of Castlereagh:
Stop, traveller, and piss.'

LORD BYRON about the grave of Lord Castlereagh,
2nd Marquess of Londonderry (1769–1822)

VERBOSE TO THE END

Meanwhile, it takes a short story rather than a pithy quip to sum up certain larger-than-life celebrities.

'In Remembrance of that Prodigy in Nature
DANIEL LAMBERT
a Native of Leicester:
who was possessed of an exalted and convivial Mind
and in personal Greatness had no Competitor
He measured three Feet one Inch round the Leg
nine Feet four Inches round the Body
and weighed
Fifty-two Stone eleven Pounds!
He departed this Life on the 21st of June 1809
Aged 39 years
As a Testimony of Respect this Stone is erected by his
Friends in Leicester.'

DANIEL LAMBERT (1770–1809),
formerly the fattest man in the world

Famous Last Words

'On the contrary!'

Known as 'the father of modern theatre', the Norwegian playwright HENRIK IBSEN'S (1828–1902) final utterance was to contradict his housekeeper's statement that he was feeling a little better. That showed her.

'Stranger
Beneath this cone in
Unconsecrated
Ground
A friend to the liberties
Of Mankind
Directed his body to be inurned
May the example contribute
To the emancipation of thy mind
From the idle fears of
Superstition
And the wicked arts
Of priesthood.'

JOHN BASKERVILLE (1706–75), typesetter and atheist

'Near this Spot
are deposited the Remains of one
who possessed Beauty without Vanity,
Strength without Insolence,
Courage without Ferocity,
and all the Virtues of Man without his Vices.
This praise, which would be unmeaning Flattery
if inscribed over human Ashes,
is but a just Tribute to the Memory of
BOATSWAIN, a DOG
who was born in Newfoundland, May 1803,
and died at Newstead, Nov. 18, 1808.'

BOATSWAIN, Lord Byron's dog,
Newstead Abbey, Nottinghamshire

Famous Last Words

'Shit.'

The single, simple last exclamation of the once effusive
American poet WALT WHITMAN (1819–92).

EPITAPHS OF THE (EXTRA-) ORDINARY

Hilarious headstones are not the sole preserve of the rich and famous, as this collection of 'ordinary' epitaphs from around the world shows.

'HERE LIES AN ATHEIST
All dressed up
and no place to go.'

'CONNECTION RESET BY PEER
He came, he saw, he logged out.'

'TWO THINGS I LOVE MOST: GOOD HORSES AND
BEAUTIFUL WOMEN
And when I die, I hope they tan this old hide of mine and
make it into a ladies' riding saddle, so I can rest in peace
between the two things I love most.'

'Here lies John Steere,
Who, when living, brewed good beer.
Turn to the right, go down the hill:
His son keeps up the business still.'

'Here lies the remains of James Pady, Brickmaker, in hope
that his clay will be remoulded in a workmanlike manner,
far superior to his former perishable materials.'

'Resurgam!
But don't tell my husband of it.'

'He rests in pieces
Now ain't that
Too bad.'

John:
'FREE YOUR BODY AND SOUL
UNFOLD YOUR POWERFUL WINGS
CLIMB UP THE HIGHEST MOUNTAINS
KICK YOUR FEET UP IN THE AIR
YOU MAY NOW LIVE FOR EVER
OR RETURN TO THIS EARTH
UNLESS YOU FEEL GOOD WHERE YOU ARE!
Missed by your friends.'

'She always said her feet were killing her,
But nobody believed her.'

'Once I wasn't
Then I was
Now I ain't again.'

'Sacred to the memory of
My husband
John Barnes
Who died January 3, 1803.
His comely young widow,
Aged 23,
Has many qualifications of a good wife,
And yearns to be comforted.'

'The pretty flowers that blossom here
Are fertilized by Gertie Greer.'

'Hurry! The party's started.'

'HERE LIES ANN MANN
Who lived an old maid
But died an old Mann.'

'HERE LIES JOHN YEAST
Pardon me for not rising.'

'I am safe in saying
She's gone up higher
Nary a devil
Would want Maria.'

'I have transplanted a large portion to heaven in acts of
charity,
And have gone thither to enjoy it.'

'Daniel E. Cole
Born Feb 2, 1844
Went Away
March 22, 1921
I wonder where he went.'

'Gone to meet his mother-in-law.'

'Underneath this crust
Lies the mouldering dust
Of Eleanor Batchelor Shoven,
Well versed in the arts
Of pies, custards and tarts,
And the lucrative trade of the oven.
When she lived long enough,
She made her last puff,
A puff by her husband much praised,
And now she doth lie
And make a dirt pie,
In hopes that her crust may be raised.'

'Underneath this pile of stones
Lies all that's left of Sally Jones
Her name was Lord, it was not Jones,
But Jones was used to rhyme with stones.'

'Here lies the body, late Mayor of Dundee
Here lies him, here lies he
ABCDEFG
Di Do Dum, Di Do Dee.'

'Shhh.'

'Those who knew him best deplored him most.'

'Her temper furious
Her tongue was vindictive
She resented a look
And frowned at a smile
And was sour as vinegar
She punished the earth
Upwards of 40 years
To say nothing of her relations.'

'He was literally a father
To all the children of the parish.'

'Faithful husband,
Thou art at rest
Until we meet again.'

'Erected to the memory of
John MacFarlane
Drowned in the water of Leith
By a few affectionate friends.'

'Here lies my wife, a sad slattern and shrew;
If I said I was sorry, I should lie too.'

'Here lie the bones of Elizabeth Charlotte,
Born a virgin, died a harlot.
For sixteen years she kept her virginity –
A damn'd long time in this vicinity.'

'JIMMY
A tiny marmoset
August 16th 1937
There isn't enough
Darkness in the world
To quench the light
Of one small candle.'

'In memory of
MAGGIE*
Who in her time kicked
Two colonels,
Four majors,
Ten captains,
Twenty-four lieutenants,
Forty-two sergeants,
Four hundred and thirty-two other ranks,
And one Mills bomb.'

* An army mule during the First World War

'I still go up my forty-four stairs two
at a time, but that is in hopes of dropping
dead at the top.'

A. E. HOUSMAN, POET

PAMPERED PUSSYCATS AND PRIZED POOCHES

Leaving the Lot to Your
Favourite Furry Friend

COUNTESS CARLOTTA'S CANINE

We've all heard tales of eccentric dog lovers leaving fortunes to their beloved four-legged companions, but the grandly named Countess Carlotta Liebenstein took it to a whole other level. She left her dog Gunther III an $80 million estate. That's right, $80 million.

Gunther's heir, Gunther IV, is currently said to live in the lap of doggie luxury with a personal maid, a chauffeur and a customized pool.

MOST HONOURED HOUSEFLY

The Roman poet Virgil (70–19 BC) held an elaborate funeral for his pet fly, spending an estimated £50,000 in today's money. The fly's ceremony was a catered affair, complete with an orchestra and even paid mourners.

When contemplating his own demise, Virgil requested that the books he had written be burned upon his death. Having only completed twelve books in his lifetime, as opposed to the twenty-four of the epic poems of Homer, he thought his work unworthy and incomplete. Thankfully his friends managed to convince him to remove the request from his will. He consented and his great poem the *Aeneid* was released to great acclaim and remains a staple on school and university curricula to this day.

Famous Last Words

'I am dying. Please, bring me a toothpick.'

Surreal to the last, these are the last words of
French absurdist playwright
ALFRED JARRY (1873–1907) inventor of *pataphysique*,
the science of imaginary solutions.

THE QUEEN
OF MEAN

Billionaire hotel tycoon Leona Helmsley, known by the rather unflattering moniker 'The Queen of Mean', was convicted for tax evasion and famously heard to say: 'We don't pay taxes. Only the little people pay taxes.' She's also well known for her elaborate generosity to her beloved menagerie of pets. Upon her death in 2007 Helmsley left the bulk of her estate, an estimated $4 billion, to her own charitable trust set up to benefit dogs. She also ensured that her beloved Trouble, a Maltese toy dog, was kept in high style with a $12 million trust fund. Predictably her family have gone out of their way to contest the will and Trouble's trust fund has been depleted to just $2 million. We are assured that this will more than cover the pampered pooch's needs for the next ten years or so, which include full-time security and a guardian fee of $160,000 a year plus an annual grooming bill of a relatively meagre $8000.

> 'I believe in reincarnation, so I've left all my money to myself.'
> TONY BLACKBURN, RADIO DJ

DOGGONE CRAZY

Eleanor Ritchey, heiress to the Quaker State Refining Corporation, has also gone down in history for her exceptional generosity to her four-legged friends. Upon her death in 1968 she willed her entire fortune of some $4.5 million to her 150 dogs. Again, the family contested the will and after a five-year court battle an agreement was reached. By that time Ritchey's estate had grown to $14 million and half of the dogs had died of natural causes. The remaining dogs were awarded $9 million, which meant that each canine received over $123,000. Ritchey's brothers and sisters were given just $2 million to divide among themselves and the rest of the estate went towards paying dog minder fees.

GONE TO THE CATHOUSE

Friend to felines Jonathan Jackson of Ohio stated in his 1880 will that: 'It is man's duty as lord of animals to watch over and protect the lesser and feebler.' To fulfil this obligation, Jackson left a substantial sum for the creation of a 'cat house' replete with comfortable sleeping quarters, a dining hall, a conversation room, an auditorium where they could listen to live accordion music, an exercise area, and a specially designed roof for easy climbing.

POOR OLD SIDO

Animal lover Mary Murphy of San Francisco generously left the bulk of her $200,000 estate to a shelter, Pets Unlimited, upon her death in 1979. But her will also contained a rather harsh clause ordering the immediate destruction of her own collie Sido. The Society for the Prevention of Cruelty to Animals (SPCA) decided to challenge her will in court and elsewhere the California Governor himself waded in – hurriedly signing a special bill that would spare the dog's life. Sido was taken into the home of the SPCA director Richard Avanzino as they'd formed a close bond during the case. What Mary Murphy had against poor old Sido we'll never know.

MONKEY BUSINESS

A Danish animal lover left her entire fortune of €67,000 to six chimpanzees housed in a Copenhagen zoo. To execute her will in accordance with the Danish law, it was read to the chimpanzees, which were named Trine, Jimmy, Trunte, Fifi, Grinni, and Gigi. Apparently they were unmoved by the news.

MUMMIFIED MOUSE

In 1979 wealthy Egyptian businessman Abdel Nahas left $2 million to his beloved pet mouse. Adding insult to his overlooked family's injury, the mouse wasn't even alive. It died and was mummified the previous year.

> 'When you've told someone that you've left them a legacy, the only decent thing to do is to die at once.'
>
> SAMUEL BUTLER, POET

BLACKIE'S IN THE BLACK

Worth a cool $25 million Blackie, the Guinness Book of Records' richest cat, did rather nicely when his owner Ben Rea died. Rea's relatives didn't get a penny when the reclusive millionaire passed away. It is sadly unknown how Blackie has spent his millions.

CHICKENFEED

Showing that it's not just dogs and cats that get all the cash, hen Gigoo is reported to be the lucky recipient of some $10 million after the death of publishing giant Miles Blackwell. Miles died just three weeks after his wife in 2002, shortly after the couple retired to indulge their life-long love of animals and rear rare pigs and chickens. It's likely that she was one of many recipients at the Rare Breeds Survival Trust, but I like to think of Gigoo stockpiling the cash all for herself.

TROPHY TORTOISE

While $27,000 isn't quite in the league of some of the other animal beneficiaries recorded here – it's still not to be sneezed at. Especially if you're a low-maintenance fifty-year-old tortoise. Named for his unusual speediness, Silverstone the tortoise was the favourite pet of bookshop tycoon Christina Foyle, owner of London's famous Foyle's bookshop.

Famous Last Words

'I wish I had drunk more champagne.'

JOHN MAYNARD KEYNES (1883–1946), the economist who lent his name to the English town 'Milton Keynes' – a place not usually associated with the high life.

Another man hankering after some bubbly on his deathbed was playwright ANTON CHEKHOV (1860–1904) who reputedly said to his wife before expiring: 'It's a long time since I drank champagne.'

IT'S ALIVE!

Faked and Mistaken Deaths

UP THE CREEK
WITHOUT A PADDLE

The Darwin Awards, named after father of evolution Charles Darwin, honour those who have improved the human gene pool by removing themselves from it in some ridiculous or idiotic manner. But it is another Darwin who surely deserves an award for the most idiotic faked death.

John Darwin, a former science teacher turned prison officer from the north of England, went missing after paddling out to sea in his canoe in early 2002. A massive search and rescue operation was mounted, but to no avail. The following day rescuers found the wreckage of Darwin's canoe. A year later, with no further leads as to the whereabouts of his body, he was officially declared dead. The small comfort to his wife, Anne, was that this verdict released a £25,000 payout from John's life insurance policy, £88,000 in various pension payments and £137,000 from his mortgage insurance policy – money that was desperately needed to pay off the couple's many thousands of pounds' worth of crippling debt.

All of this presumably came as something of a relief to John Darwin, who had in fact been living in a bedsit next door to the family home since the day of his supposed demise. A secret hole in the wall behind a wardrobe allowed him to move between the two properties and to hide when his wife received condoling visitors. During one particularly

90

spectacular lapse in vigilance, Darwin bumped into a neighbour in the stairwell of the block of bedsits. 'Aren't you supposed to be dead?' asked the neighbour. 'Don't tell anyone about this,' Darwin insisted.

Keeping a low profile proved difficult for Darwin, and he and Anne spent the next few years travelling around the world, thanks to a passport he had obtained under a false identity. They toyed with the idea of buying property in various exotic locations and even put down a deposit on a luxury £45,000 boat. Having settled on Panama, the Darwins sold their British homes and put the money towards an ambitious project to set up an eco-hotel offering, of all things, canoeing holidays.

But all of this subterfuge and jetsetting seemed to have taken its toll by December 2007, when John Darwin wandered into a London police station claiming to have no memory of the previous five years. 'I think I am a missing person,' he said. The world's press was gripped by this miraculous reappearance and Anne, who was at her home in Panama, was reported to be over the moon. But a cynical and tech-savvy member of the British public single-handedly proved that all was not as it seemed by googling 'John Anne Panama' and finding a photo of the couple, dated 2006, on the website of a Panamanian real estate company.

With their story unravelling faster than they could cope with, the Darwins had to hand themselves in. At trial in 2008 John Darwin admitted to, and was convicted of, obtaining money by deception and a passport by fraudulent means. Both he and Anne were imprisoned, but released in early 2011.

'It's funny how most people love the dead.
Once you're dead, you're made for life.'

JIMI HENDRIX, rock legend (died tragically at the age of
twenty-seven and his record sales skyrocketed).

TRIAL RUN

Timothy Dexter – aka Lord Timothy Dexter or the Marquis
of Newburyport, as he liked to be known – was an eccentric
eighteenth-century Massachusetts businessman. His business
interests were as eclectic as his personality: over the years he
traded in women's accessories, whalebone, warming pans,
West Indian produce, property and financial securities. His
home was adorned with minarets and golden embellishments
and surrounded by a gaggle of larger-than-life statues of the
likes of George Washington, Thomas Jefferson, Napoleon
Bonaparte, William Pitt, Horatio Nelson, King George IV,
Benjamin Franklin – and two of Dexter himself, one of which
proclaimed him 'the greatest philosopher in the Western
world'. He declared his former apprentice the poet laureate of
his domain, kitted him out in official livery and crowned him
with a wreath of parsley.

Dexter's own literary ambitions were realized with the
publication in 1802 of his autobiographical *A Pickle for*

the Knowing Ones, which was purposefully misspelled throughout and contained absolutely no punctuation. A page of commas, full stops and question marks was provided at the back of the book for the reader to 'peper and soolt' the text himself.

In his later years, Dexter's pride and joy was the mausoleum he had had made for himself in the summer house, complete with outrageously expensive coffin. In order to fine-tune the details of his inevitable death, he had it put about that he had died and that everyone was invited to the funeral. His long-suffering family played along with the ruse, dressing up in black and welcoming the townspeople to the property. A sermon and emotional eulogy were delivered and the coffin taken in procession to its final resting place, after which everyone was invited back to the mansion for a feast. It was during the solemn festivities that guests overheard some sort of altercation in the kitchen and rushed in to find 'Lord' Dexter thrashing his wife with a cane for not having wept sufficiently at the funeral.

'Lady' Dexter's substandard acting skills aside, the dry run was declared a roaring success, although when Dexter really did die in 1806 he was buried in a communal graveyard beneath a simple headstone.

ONE FLEW OVER THE MEXICAN BORDER

American author Ken Kesey, whose most famous novel, *One Flew Over the Cuckoo's Nest*, was made into an Oscar-winning movie of the same name, was so determined not to be busted for his infamous enthusiasm for illegal substances that he faked his own death.

As well as writing his bestselling novel, which was published in 1962, Kesey spent the early 1960s taking part in clinical trials for various hallucinogenic drugs. He subsequently formed a group called the Merry Pranksters and they drove across America in a psychedelic-themed converted schoolbus named Further, introducing as many people as possible to the wonders of LSD.

In 1965, however, Kesey was arrested in California for possession of marijuana. In order to avoid imprisonment he got the Merry Pranksters to place a lengthy suicide note inside his van and abandon it at the edge of a cliff. By the time the vehicle was discovered, Kesey was on his way to Mexico in the boot of another friend's car.

After eight months on the wrong side of death, Kesey returned to America and was thrown in jail for five months. He died in 2001.

> 'Death is not the end. There remains the litigation over the estate.'
>
> AMBROSE BIERCE, SATIRIST

THE LUCKY LORD

One of the most infamous faked deaths of the twentieth century is all the more infamous for remaining a total mystery. Indeed, nobody knows whether the person in question is in fact currently dead or alive. But he certainly had good reason to vanish.

Richard Bingham, 7th Earl of Lucan, aka Lord Lucan or Lucky Lucan, disappeared off the face of the earth on

8 November 1974, effectively incriminating himself for a violent murder that had taken place the previous evening at the London home of his estranged wife, and which he is still officially presumed to have committed.

Two months earlier, Lady Lucan had hired a nanny, Sandra Rivett, to look after her three children. On the night in question, according to her subsequent statement, Lady Lucan was watching television when it suddenly dawned on her that Ms Rivett was taking an awfully long time to make a promised cup of tea. She went to the basement kitchen to look for her but found the room in total darkness. She called the nanny's name, at which point a man emerged from the shadows and attacked her with a lead pipe. During the altercation she recognized the assailant as her estranged husband, who eventually revealed that Sandra Rivett was dead.

With the children still upstairs, Lady Lucan – thought to be the intended target of Lucan's murderous rage – was able to subdue her husband, but she fled the house as soon as he set about cleaning the mess. Covered in blood, she burst into the nearest pub, screaming, 'Help me, help me, help me! I've just escaped from being murdered! He's in the house – he's killed the nanny!' By the time the police arrived at the house, Lord Lucan was gone. Sandra Rivett's body was in a sack in the basement.

During the next few hours, Lucan made a series of erratic phone calls and visits to friends' houses, at no point admitting any responsibility for the scene of carnage at the family home. He was never seen again – aside, of course, from numerous supposed sightings around the world, including a 2007 appearance in New Zealand as a homeless man living in a Land Rover with a cat, a possum and a goat. He was officially declared dead *in absentia* in 1999, at the age of sixty-five.

A TOWERING IDIOT

Of all the terrible and terrifying stories to emerge from the 9/11 atrocity in New York, two accounts provided a very welcome spot of comic relief.

Shortly after the attacks, a bereaved man provided documentation in support of a death certificate application for his brother, Steven Chin Leung, who had been working for the brokerage Cantor Fitzgerald in the World Trade Center, and who was now missing, presumed dead. Suspicions were raised when it emerged that Steven Chin Leung did not have a brother and that the email 'proof' of his employment was fabricated.

The man applying for the death certificate was, in fact, Steven Chin Leung himself. The Hong Kong national was in trouble with the authorities in Hawaii for passport fraud, and he hoped that his tragic demise might convince them to drop the charge. Instead of a period of probation for the passport swindle, he was sentenced to four years in jail for his 'extraordinary efforts to take advantage of a national tragedy'.

Unbelievably, he was not the only one to do so. Mother and daughter Dorothy Johnson and Twila McKee were arrested and charged in August 2003 with insurance fraud and attempted theft, after alleging that Johnson had died in the attacks. All in all they had attempted to claim $135,000 in life insurance and associated benefits. The pair were clearly not seasoned criminals, however: not only did Johnson leave fingerprints on the letter informing her insurance company of her own death, but she also apparently forgot about the insurance claim she had made in relation to a car accident that occurred twelve days after 9/11.

Famous Last Words

'Am I dying or is this my birthday?'

Thus spoke the eighty-five-year-old LADY ASTOR (1879–1964) when she awoke on her deathbed to find herself surrounded by her family. She was the first female member of parliament in the UK and was known for her witty turns of phrase. On the subject of women's rights she famously said: 'We are not asking for superiority for we have always had that; all we ask is equality.'

ALL AT SEA

In November 1974, British Labour politician John Stonehouse realized he was in a bit of a pickle. His political fortunes were up and down, he had resorted to 'creative accounting' in an attempt to keep his various failing businesses afloat, he was having an extramarital affair with his secretary, and he had been accused – correctly, it later transpired – of being a spy for the Soviets.

The MP concluded that this 'John Stonehouse' character was, all things considered, a total disaster, and he resolved to turn his life around by taking on a new identity. Adopting the name Joseph Markham – the deceased husband of one of his constituents – he spent time practising the role of an 'honest' individual when out and about on his own, before mounting an ambitious attempt to switch personas for good.

On 20 November 1974, Stonehouse left a pile of clothes on Miami Beach and disappeared, leaving police to come to the obvious conclusion that he had drowned. He was in fact in Australia with his secretary, having obtained a false passport under his new name. Ironically, although he needed to engage in complex financial fraud to gain access to his savings, Stonehouse's transactions only raised the alarm because an Australian bank teller suspected he might be the fugitive Lord Lucan, who had mysteriously disappeared a fortnight earlier!

John Stonehouse was arrested in Australia on Christmas Eve 1974 and deported back to the UK the following summer. He was sentenced to seven years' imprisonment for fraud, at which point his long-suffering wife realized it was high time she divorced him. He married his former secretary after his release and continued to work in politics until his death in 1988.

> 'I have nothing against undertakers personally. It's just that I wouldn't want one to bury my sister.'
>
> JESSICA MITFORD, author, journalist and 'Mitford sister'

HEAD IN THE CLOUDS

While most faked deaths involve the 'deceased' disappearing without a trace, the drama, derring-do and indeed stupidity of this particular story are worthy of a Hollywood movie.

Until 2007 Marcus Schrenker was a wealthy Indiana investment adviser who enjoyed the kinds of luxuries that most people can only dream of: among other things, a collection of expensive cars, a private plane and a model wife. But 2008 got off to a terrible start for him when he was accused by several clients of having misled them. Over the course of the year his home was raided and he was hauled into court and subsequently charged with unlawful acts. In December his wife filed for divorce, having discovered that he was having an affair.

Schrenker desperately needed to escape from this downward spiral and so he hatched what appeared to be an ingenious plan. In early January 2009 he set off in his propeller plane en route to Florida, but halfway there he made a distress call in which he claimed that the plane's windshield had imploded and that he was bleeding heavily. He then put the plane on autopilot, leapt from the cockpit with a parachute, made his way to a garage in Alabama where he had left his motorbike and some money, and escaped into the sunset.

It would all have been so perfect had it not been for the military jets that were scrambled to intercept Schrenker's 'troubled' plane and which found it soaring happily through the air with the cockpit door open. When it crash-landed in northern Florida, within sight of residential buildings, investigators confirmed that there had been nothing wrong with the plane and that there was no evidence of injury to the missing pilot, but they did find maps and campsite guides whose Alabama and Florida pages had been torn out.

Schrenker, meanwhile, was doing a terrible job of keeping his head down. A series of far-fetched stories and cash payments roused the suspicions of the people he encountered, and it only took a few simple phone calls to local campsites for the police to locate the fugitive's tent in Quincy, Florida. He is currently serving time for charges relating to the plane crash and financial fraud.

A FATE WORSE THAN DEATH

Faced with crippling debts, a handful of enterprising people have faked their own deaths in order to avoid having to cough up. But two men on either side of the Atlantic showed extraordinary dedication to the cause when they claimed to have died to get off relatively piddling fines.

In Lancashire in 2007, unlucky motorist Shafkat Munir received three speeding tickets and a demand for £180 in fines. In order to avoid paying he posed as a friend and called the police to inform them that Shafkat had sadly passed away in Pakistan five years earlier. He even forged a death certificate in slightly dodgy Urdu. When police examined the speed cameras, however, they saw that the man behind the wheel was without doubt the dear departed; when they called his mobile phone, he admitted his real identity. He was sentenced to a year's imprisonment and banned from driving for eighteen months. 'I have never known anyone go to such lengths,' said a representative of the local Road Safety Partnership. 'Munir's license was clean before this spate of incidents and he would still have been able to drive.'

Around the same time in Chicago, Illinois, Corey Taylor was swearing at his latest defective mobile phone and plotting a way of getting out of his two-year contract without incurring the standard $175 fee. Naturally he decided the only thing for it was to fake his own death. 'I thought, "What have I got to lose, besides a cellphone I despise?"' he explained after the company in question failed to fall for the fake death certificate they received by fax.

NICE TRY

Faking one's death is quite an ambitious undertaking, but most fakers are at least rewarded by having news of their terrible demise believed for a short while. Not so American hedge fund manager Samuel Israel III, who faked suicide in 2008 as a means of escaping a twenty-year prison sentence for his part in a $450 million fraud.

He set the scene pretty well: his car was found abandoned on a bridge over the Hudson River, with the words 'Suicide is Painless' – the theme song, incidentally, for the hit TV show *M*A*S*H* – scrawled in dust on the bonnet. Israel was nowhere to be seen.

But the FBI was having none of it. Why? Well, for one thing, the 'suicide note' was surrounded by pine needles, of which there was an abundance in Israel's driveway but none near the bridge. Secondly, nobody had seen anyone leap into the water; indeed, witnesses claimed to have seen someone being picked up from the bridge in a second car. Finally they figured that a man who had had the swagger to run a $450 million 'Ponzi' scheme probably had the swagger to fake his own death in order to get away with it.

The final nail in the fake coffin was Israel's girlfriend's confession of her role in the suicide scam, and after three weeks on the run, he turned himself in. In light of his time-wasting escapades, the judge increased his prison sentence to twenty-two years.

Famous Last Words

'They couldn't hit an elephant
at this distance.'

The sadly ironic last words of GENERAL JOHN
SEDGWICK (1813–64) shot in the face by seemingly far
off Confederate soldiers at the 'Battle of the Wilderness'.

KEEP CALM
AND
CARRY ON

When Singapore resident Gandaruban Subramaniam decided to go on the run from the illegal money lenders and creditors who had been propping up his failed business, he certainly did so in style. Not content to 'fall into the ocean' like most other fakers, Subramaniam got his family to claim he had been killed by Tamil Tigers in a dramatic civil war shoot-out in Sri Lanka in 1987.

With $250,000 in life insurance and a fake passport to hand, Subramaniam spent twenty years coming and going between Sri Lanka and Singapore, even marrying his 'widowed' wife in 1994 and fathering their fourth child.

His luck eventually ran out, however, and he was arrested at Singapore's Changi Airport in 2007 after using his fake passport one too many times.

> 'When I am dead, I hope it may be said:
> "His sins were scarlet,
> but his books were read."'
>
> HILAIRE BELLOC, POET

WILLING AND ABEL

Alan Abel is a career prankster who earned notoriety in the 1950s for such hoaxes as the Society for Indecency to Naked Animals, a faux-moral crusade whose mission was to clothe all animals for the sake of propriety (slogan: A Nude

Horse is a Rude Horse). It whipped the media into a frenzy of outrage but had members of the public devising knitting patterns for animal fashion.

Abel's most daring stunt, however, came in late 1979, when he created an elaborate story surrounding his supposed death in a skiing accident. Having hired an actor to dress as a funeral director and collect his belongings from the ski lodge, he had a woman claiming to be his wife notify the New York Times that Alan Abel had died while scouting locations for a forthcoming film called *Who's Going to Bite Your Neck, Dear, When All of My Teeth Are Gone?*

The stunt was deemed a roaring success when the *New York Times* printed his obituary – the whole purpose of the hoax – and Abel was able to come back to life the following morning at a press conference.

WAKEY, WAKEY, RIP

Very few people can claim to have read their own obituary in *The Times*, but there is perhaps only one person who has had the dubious honour of seeing news of his death followed a year later by news of his marriage.

When staff at *The Times* were updating former BBC commentator Rex Alston's rolling obituary in 1985, they accidentally sent it off to be published rather than archived. As a result the eighty-four-year-old, who in an unfortunate twist of fate had been hospitalized the previous evening, was treated to some rather alarming breakfast reading.

Nonetheless, Alston remarried the following year and lived into his nineties.

POSTHUMOUS PROTESTER

Indian farmer Lal Bihari was inspired to establish the Association of the Dead – an organization that fights to reinstate people erroneously declared dead by greedy relatives working in collusion with corrupt officials – when he went to apply for a bank loan and discovered that he was officially deceased. It transpired that his uncle had declared him dead in order to steal his land.

Bihari remained dead between 1976 and 1994, during which time he engaged in a series of high-profile pranks in an attempt to prove he was alive. He arranged his own funeral and tried to claim widow's insurance for his wife; he took to signing his name 'Lal Bihari Mritak' ('the late Lal Bihari'); and he even ran for office against Prime Minister Rajiv Gandhi.

Finally, in 1994, the authorities relented and admitted that he did indeed appear to be alive. In 2003 he was awarded the tongue-in-cheek Ig Nobel Peace Prize – which aims to 'make people laugh, and then make them think' – for 'leading an active life even though he has been declared legally dead'.

OUCH!

When Carlos Camejo was killed in a road accident in Venezuela in 2007, his terrible day was only just beginning.

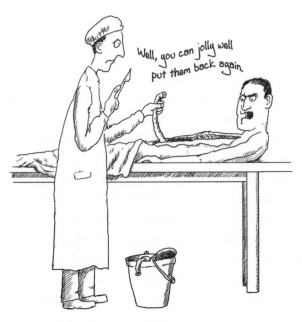

The body was taken straight to a local morgue, where medical examiners began carrying out an autopsy, when suddenly the dead man awoke. Fortunately the doctors had got no further than making an incision on his face.

'I woke up because the pain was unbearable,' Camejo told a newspaper. With any luck his wife's reaction when she came to identify his body and found him sitting in the corridor made up for it.

FORGOTTEN, BUT NOT GONE

In April 2003, a technical glitch revealed that the half-written obituaries for numerous living world leaders were floating around on the CNN website. The embarrassing debacle exposed not only that CNN was already anticipating various high-profile deaths, but also that it had a habit of using tried-and-tested obituaries as templates for newer departures.

For some reason, the obituary of the Queen Mother had proved particularly inspirational, as a result of which Vice President Dick Cheney was gushingly referred to as the 'UK's Favorite Grandmother'. Readers could click through to sections on his love of horse racing and his life as Queen Consort. Fidel Castro, meanwhile, had been grafted into the obituary for Ronald Reagan, and was glowingly described as a 'lifeguard, athlete and movie star'.

Famous Last Words

'I've had a helluva lot of fun, and I've enjoyed every minute of it.'

Pretty much everyone's dream last words –
in this case uttered by the original man in tights, the
roguish ERROL FLYNN (1909–59). He's also quoted
as saying, 'I shall return.'

STRANGER THAN FICTION

At breakfast in a hotel one morning in 1816, poet Samuel Taylor Coleridge overheard his name being mentioned in relation to a coroner's inquest. He looked over to see a man reading a newspaper report to a friend. When asked, the man handed the paper over to Coleridge, remarking that it was an extraordinary turn of events for the writer to have killed himself so soon after the success of his new play.

'But,' added the man, 'he was always a strange mad fellow.'

'Indeed, sir,' Coleridge is said to have replied, 'it is a most extraordinary thing that he should have hanged himself, be the subject of an inquest, and yet that he should at this moment be speaking to you.'

It transpired that a man wearing one of Coleridge's shirts – presumably stolen – had been found hanged in London's Hyde Park.

> 'Picasso was a delightful, kindly, friendly, simple little man. When I met him he was extremely excited and overjoyed that his mother-in-law had just died, and he was looking forward to the funeral.'
>
> EDITH SITWELL, DAME AND POET

THE BEST 'BACK FROM THE DEAD' FILM MOMENTS

Even though the evil nutter always gets their comeuppance at the end of the film, you can't help feeling they've had the last laugh, not least because of the trail of destruction left in their wake ... and the fact that they're about to make a miraculous comeback for the sequel! Here's a selection of some of the best 'back from the dead' moments in film history. Many of them would give Rasputin a run for his money ...

Halloween (1978–)

This first 1978 slasher featured the debut of Jamie Lee Curtis as Laurie, the virginal victim of the murderous mask-wearing lunatic Michael Myers – who, of course, turns out to be her half brother. Now here is a villain who just won't quit.

Over ten bloodthirsty films Myers manages to escape mental asylums, repeatedly defy death and 'come back from the dead' with spectacular regularity. At the end of the first film, Michael is shot seven times by his psychiatrist after a night of rampaging, house-to-house menacing and murdering female babysitters. The second film picks up where the first left off, but Michael's body is missing – it turns out he's alive and follows Laurie to the hospital where he continues rampaging until he is ultimately engulfed in flames.

More recently he's been resurrected in remakes of the first two films. If and when he'll ever die is anyone's guess.

The original *Halloween* was produced on a budget of $320,000 and grossed $47.3 million at the box office in the United States, plus the sequels and royalties ensure that creator John Carpenter will most definitely have the last laugh.

Sleeping with the Enemy (1991)

In this 1991 film a doe-eyed Julia Roberts (Laura) fakes her own death to escape her controlling, violent, obsessive-compulsive husband and goes off to start a new life in an all-American town. Ten minutes later she's falling for her hunky/hairy next-door neighbour. But it's not long till her evil husband discovers that not only is she in fact still breathing, worse, she's not arranging various items in her new house the way he'd like.

When Laura returns home one day, she finds an elaborate series of clues that her hubby's on to her. In the bathroom she sees – horror of horrors – that her towels have been arranged in an orderly fashion. Then in the kitchen, all her jars and tins are arranged in neat rows with the labels all facing outwards. Does his cruelty know no end?

Having sufficiently spooked her, Laura's husband announces himself by playing a haunting piece of classical musical on a ghetto blaster he appears to have brought specially. After a pretty brief scuffle Laura manages to shoot him twice. When he inevitably rises from death for one last attempt to vanquish her, she dispatches him with a third bullet and a quip.

Fatal Attraction (1987)

This film single-handedly coined the term 'bunny boiler', warning us that single women nearing forty are all potential homicidal stalkers.

Glenn Close stars as Alex, the aforementioned homicidal stalker who becomes irrationally obsessed with married man Dan (Michael Douglas). When Dan rebuffs her after a casual fling, Alex takes matters into her own hands – determined to dispatch anyone who gets in her way. First, she pours acid on his fancy car. Next, bunny gets it. In the film's most memorable and disturbing scene we find Dan's little daughter's bunny dead and boiling, fur and all, in a pot on his stove.

Not taking the hint that he's dealing with a serious loon, Dan goes around to Alex's apartment threatening and ultimately attacking her. Big mistake.

Back at Dan's house, his wife is preparing a bath when loony Alex lunges at her with a knife, Dan returns home to screaming and manages to drown Alex in the bath. Obviously, he foolishly assumes she's dead. Alex springs from the bath for one last swing of her knife before being shot by Dan's wife.

Single White Female (1992)

Another film warning against the evils of not being in a relationship, *Single White Female* stars Jennifer Jason Leigh (Hedy) and Brigitte Fonda (Allie) as flatmates whose domestic relations are strained when it becomes clear that one of them is a complete nutter. When Allie breaks up with her boyfriend she decides she could do with some female company so advertises to share her fancy city pad with a fellow 'single white female' – the seemingly nice, but frankly unhinged, Hedy.

It's not long before her new best friend is stealing Allie's look, getting her hair cut like hers, dressing like her, etc. Things come to a head when Allie gets back with her cheating boyfriend. Hedy's having none of it. Like Glenn Close before her she takes it out on a defenceless animal, killing the little puppy she bought Allie as a gift.

In an exhilarating climax – involving the gruesome murder of Allie's boyfriend with a stiletto shoe, the murder of a colleague who comes calling at an inopportune moment, and a creepy basement game of hide and seek – Allie manages to overpower the rabid Hedy. But of course, once is not enough. You just can't keep a good murderer down.

The Terminator (1984–)

When cyborg Arnold Schwarzenegger said, 'I'll be back' in the first *Terminator* movie he really meant it. The film franchise centres on a series of unstoppable machines intent on wiping out humans in the past, to stop them realizing their future destinies. The machines – or Terminators – are determined killers, programmed to fight on until their mission is completed. They are moral-free zones (except Arnold as the 'good' Terminator in the second and third films), but despite their seeming inhumanity they are partial to the occasional deadpan quip, which always assures them the last laugh. Think 'Hasta la vista, baby.'

In the first film, the joyless Arnold was shot countless times, caught in an oil tanker blast, had a pipe bomb jammed in his ribs which blew off his legs and one of his arms – but that didn't stop him! Stripped of its human skin, his chrome skeleton pulled itself towards its intended victim, Sarah Connor, with its one remaining good arm and was finally deactivated when crushed in a hydraulic press.

The trajectory of each film is a basic struggle to escape from or kill these ruthless killing machines. And they take some serious killing, but then again, so do the human protagonists.

'I'm very pleased to be here. Let's face it: at my age I'm very pleased to be anywhere.'

GEORGE BURNS, COMEDIAN

PIMP MY COFFIN

Signature Sarcophagi
for the Ultimate Send-off

BUSINESS AS USUAL

The Ga people of Ghana have a strikingly unconventional attitude towards coffins. They believe that the afterlife is pretty much 'business as usual' for the deceased, and that the dear departed are best sent on their way in a manner befitting their profession.

A fisherman, for instance, might be dispatched in a fish-shaped or boat-shaped coffin, a student in a pencil, a grocer in an enormous pineapple, a seamstress in a sewing machine, and an architect in a scaled-down replica of the Pompidou Centre in Paris. Some of the more playful designs of recent years have included an enormous Coca-Cola bottle, a private jet, a mobile phone and a huge shoe.

These bespoke coffins cost far more than most workers can afford but it is a matter not only of principle but also of pride for families to see the dead off in style. Given the inevitability of having to fork out for a funeral whether they can afford it or not, the Ga motto seems very much to be: in for a penny, in for a pound.

SEALED WITH A KISS

While fanatical music lovers will go to any lengths to secure tickets to see their favourite bands in concert, it takes a whole new level of obsession to want to be buried in a band-branded coffin. But diehard fans of American rock band Kiss are in for a treat as the group's official merchandise includes the iconic Kiss Kasket, a coffin emblazoned with the Kiss logo and the faces of all four band members.

Launched in 2001 and discontinued amid screams of protest in 2008, the Kiss Kasket made a triumphant comeback in 2011 with a sleek new design. The Standard Kasket is a relatively modest affair: a black coffin with black lining, the band logo inside and out, and the rockers' elegantly painted faces staring solemnly towards the heavens. The Premium Kasket, on the other hand, is a far bolder statement of adoration: flames lick at the semi-naked singers, who are pictured wielding guitars and axes and sporting their trademark mad expressions.

Is it worth spending multiple thousands of dollars on a Kiss Kasket you won't really be in any state to appreciate? Absolutely, say the band: buy while stocks last and put the watertight coffin to excellent use as a beer cooler for parties and other special occasions.

Famous Last Words

'I've never felt better.'

These words of reassurance were spoken by
DOUGLAS FAIRBANKS (1883–1939), 'The King of Silent
Hollywood', to his nurse as he recuperated at home
having suffered a heart attack at the age of just fifty-seven.

FUNERAL FUN

Vic Fearn & Company had been a respected Nottingham coffin-making business for well over one hundred years by the time a woman knocked on the door with a half-built aeroplane coffin and asked them to finish it off. What started as a favour for a customer in need quickly turned into a popular sideline, and when a tabloid paper ran a story on the company under the headline 'Crazy Coffins', a new company name was born.

Crazy Coffins' customers tend to have incredibly detailed requests: a specific model of Ferrari, a replica of a particular Viking boat, a glass coffin modelled on the one from *Sleeping Beauty*. Good thing, then, that most of the customers are living people placing orders for their own caskets, since these personalized designs can take weeks to make.

According to the craftsmen at Crazy Coffins, certain customers hope to sum up their personalities through a unique design while others just want to 'cause a stir'. Presumably it was the latter motivation that was behind one man's request for a very realistic-looking skip to house his remains, and another man's decision to take his glass-topped coffin home and put it to good use as a coffee table.

> 'My grandmother was a very tough woman. She buried three husbands and two of them were just napping.'
>
> RITA RUDNER, COMEDIENNE

COFFINS, COFFINS EVERYWHERE

Taking the fad for personalized coffins to new extremes, one American company has turned its hand to creating coffins for all occasions, including coffins as jewellery, coffins as carry-on luggage, coffins as contact-lens cases, coffins as bookshelves and coffins as, well, coffins.

Coffin It Up is the brainchild of an artist and cabinetmaker named Bryan who saw a gap in the market for coffin-shaped goods and has dedicated himself to filling it. Perhaps his most ambitious project to date has been the total refitting of one customer's kitchen. What she asked for was a solid maple kitchen with a rustic feel; what she got was a kitchen fitted almost entirely with coffin-shaped cabinets and surfaces, complete with hand-carved spiders' webs over the doorways. 'As you can see,' says the company website proudly, 'this kitchen is "to die for"'.

Famous Last Words

'You will show my head to the people –
it is worth seeing.'

Thus spoke GEORGES JACQUES DANTON (1759–94) to
his executioner. The Parisian lawyer had dared question
the 'Reign of Terror' wrought in the aftermath of the French
Revolution and was punished accordingly.

SEE YOU LATER ALLIGATOR (IN A WHILE CROCODILE)

The Finest and Funniest Funeral Songs

When it comes to a song to send off their loved ones, most folk err on the side of cheesy or emotive. Some, however, like to leave them laughing. Here's a list of some of the most popular funeral songs and some favourite 'alternative' tracks, and their often inappropriate lyrics, too …

TRADITIONAL TEAR-JERKERS …

'Angels' – Robbie Williams
(the number one wedding song too, bizarrely)

'Tears in Heaven' – Eric Clapton

'My Way' – Frank Sinatra

'Wind Beneath My Wings' – Bette Midler

'My Heart Will Go On' – Celine Dion

'I Will Always Love You' – Whitney Houston
(or Dolly Parton's original for Country and Western fans)

'Simply the Best' – Tina Turner

'Candle in the Wind' – Elton John

'Unchained Melody' – The Righteous Brothers

'Bridge Over Troubled Water' – Simon and Garfunkel

'Time to Say Goodbye' – Andrea Bocelli and Sarah
Brightman

'You'll Never Walk Alone' – Gerry and the Pacemakers
(especially popular at Liverpool funerals)

'We'll Meet Again' – Vera Lynn

'Without You' – Nilsson for aficionados, Mariah Carey for
everyone else

CREMATION CLASSICS . . .

'Disco Inferno' – The Trammps
('Burn baby burn')

'Light My Fire' – The Doors
('our love becomes a funeral pyre')

'Ring of Fire' – Johnny Cash
('I went down and flames went higher /
And it burns, burns, burns . . .')

'Burn in Hell' – Twisted Sister
(the words 'burn in hell' repeated a lot)

LITERAL LAST GOODBYES . . .

'Going Underground' – The Jam
('But I want nothing this society's got / I'm going
underground')

'DEAD!' – My Chemical Romance
('And if your heart stops beating / I'll be here wondering /
Did you get what you deserve?')

'Another One Bites the Dust' – Queen

'There She Goes' – The La's

'(I Just) Died In Your Arms Tonight' – Cutting Crew

> 'Death is always a great pity of course but it's not as if the alternative were immortality.'
>
> TOM STOPPARD, PLAYWRIGHT

DEFINITELY DEAD?

'Staying Alive' – The Bee Gees
('Got the wings of heaven on my shoes / I'm a dancing man
and I just can't lose.')

'Zombie' – The Cranberries

'Alive and Kicking' – Simple Minds

Famous Last Words

'My mother did it.'

ARNOLD ROTHSTEIN (1882–1928) humorously suggested his mother gunned him down rather than finger the executioners who shot him in a New York hotel room in 1928. In life Rothstein liked to say that the only thing he could fix was the weather. He was notorious for allegedly fixing the 1919 Black Sox World Series but was never convicted of a single crime.

ASSORTED FOND AND FUNNY FAREWELLS . . .

'You're as Cold as Ice' – Foreigner

'Always Look on the Bright Side of Life' – Monty Python
('For life is quite absurd / And death's the final word /
You must always face the curtain with a bow /
Forget about your sin – give the audience a grin /
Enjoy it – it's your last chance anyhow.')

'Don't Fear the Reaper' – The Blue Oyster Cult

'Return to Sender' – Elvis

'See You Later Alligator (In a While Crocodile)' – Bill Haley
and His Comets
('See you later alligator / After 'while crocodile /
Can't you see you're in my way now /
Don't you know you cramp my style.')

'Ding Dong the Witch is Dead' – The Wizard of Oz
('Wake up sleepy head, rub your eyes, get out of bed /
Wake up, the Wicked Witch is dead. She's gone where the
goblins go / Below – below – below …')

'Good Riddance (Time of Your Life)' – Green Day

'Monkey Gone to Heaven' – Pixies

'Heaven Knows I'm Miserable Now' – The Smiths
('In my life / Why do I give valuable time /
To people who don't care if I live or die?')

'When I came back to Dublin I was court-
martialled in my absence and sentenced to
death in my absence, so I said they could
shoot me in my absence.'
BRENDAN BEHAN, PLAYWRIGHT

MAKE YOUR MEMORIAL TRULY MEMORABLE

Top Ten Stylish So Longs

Humans have always been partial to a funeral and more specifically to burying our dead. Anecdotal evidence suggests we've been doing it for 200,000 years and that perhaps even the much-derided Neanderthals did it before us.

We've marked graves with mounds of earth, temples, catacombs and most recently the gravestone, which is now the norm across most of the world (though cremation is mandatory in Japan and usual in India). Some folks really go in for coffins, while others prefer a 'natural' burial – in which the body is returned to the soil sans casket. Mummification was once quite the thing, and mausoleums or family crypts are the preferred choice of burial for those who can afford them. Or, if you're really fancy you might get entombed in a church.

Sometimes we bury gifts and goods with our dearly departed, sometimes dress them up in their Sunday best and sometimes strip them bare. Sometimes we bury our dead on their backs, on their fronts, in the foetal position, or facing Mecca. Sometimes we bury our dead singly, other times in the same plot as loved ones. Sometimes if we're not keen on the person we're burying or they've committed suicide we bury them upside down or at a crossroads. Sometimes we bury our dead en masse in 'potter's fields', unidentified and without much dignity.

UNDERGROUND, OVERGROUND

For the belligerent or the barmy among us, there are plenty of ways we can ensure that our funerals make a big impression on those we leave behind. Here are my top-ten suggestions for a glorious (or inglorious) send-off, drawing on some unusual death rites from around the globe.

Sky burial

The ultimate in eco-friendly corpse disposable, the sky burial really does give something back to nature. A common funeral rite in Tibet, the deceased's remains are deposited on top of a mountain, exposed to the elements and hungry birds of prey.

Famous Last Words

'Drink to me!'

PABLO PICASSO (1881–1973). A fitting farewell from the ninety-one-year-old bon viveur and ground-breaking artist, known for paying his bills by cheque, safe in the knowledge that they'd never be banked because of the value of his signature.

Burning boat

Not so popular any more, this was the one-time favourite disposal method of the Vikings. Given the labour involved in making a boat millennia ago, it's not surprising that only the highest-profile Vikings got to go out to sea on a fiery one. Of course, these days there are plenty of cheaper options – rubber dinghies, canoes, peddle boats, punts – all you need is some open water and some lighter fluid.

Hired mourners

Whether you're being picked clean on a hillside or burned on a boat, the ostentatious among you should really consider hiring some professional mourners for your special day. Popular in Roman times and, until recently, rural Ireland, hired wailers add that extra theatricality to proceedings, making your final send-off one to remember.

> 'I'm always relieved when someone is delivering a eulogy and I realize I'm listening to it.'
> GEORGE CARLIN, COMEDIAN

Space burial

Not the cheapest option, but with the advance of technology and rising demand, the space burial will soon be an option that suits everyone's pocket.

So far 250 or so people are known to have had their cremated remains shot into space, far enough so that they'll circle the Earth for at least 200 years before coming back down with a bang.

Famous sky-burial participants include Gene Roddenberry, creator of *Star Trek*, and Timothy Leary, LSD advocate. It's one hell of a trip!

Hanging coffins

If you're not quite ready to disappear from view, you might want to consider the hanging coffin option, popular in rural China and the Philippines. Usually placed on the vertical face of a mountain, jutting from a cave mouth or balanced on a rock formation, the hanging coffin is the perfect option for people who want to ensure they're not forgotten. (See page 147 – 'Hang loose')

Famadihana

If you fancy more than one funeral then Madagascar's Famadihana ritual should be right up your street. Known as turning the bones, this tradition has only been around 200 to 300 years and involves family members disinterring their ancestors to rewrap them in fresh cloth, then having a second funeral party – dancing with the corpses around the tomb to live music.

'My dear, before you kiss me goodbye, fix your hair. It's a mess.'

Pulitzer prizewinning playwright, GEORGE KELLY (1887–1974), to his unkempt niece on his deathbed.

Sokushunbutsu

Or if you're really into DIY then there's the Japanese Buddhist practice of Sokushunbutsu. Basically self-mummification, Sokushunbutsu involves extreme self-denial and self-poisoning, until all body fat and bodily fluids have been sapped away – then with your last bit of strength crawling into a box and assuming the lotus position until death. The box is then sealed and – all being well – a perfectly mummified corpse will remain within.

Ritual cannibalism

It's a lot to ask, granted. But getting your nearest and dearest to cannibalize you will certainly make for a memorable send-off.

It's a lot more common in human history then you'd think. Rumours abound that the people of Papua New Guinea still cannibalize their dead in time-honoured fashion.

We assume that practitioners want to absorb the strength, bravery, wisdom and other attributes of the deceased by eating their heart, liver or brain – rather than just being a bit peckish.

The Yanomami tribe of the Venezuelan-Brazilian rainforest are known to eat the cremated ashes of their dearly departed mixed up with banana paste. Tasty.

Plastination

Perfected by German Gunther von Hagens in the late 1970s, plastination is an innovative way of preserving human flesh for all to see. His recent controversial touring show 'Body Worlds' displayed hundreds of donated bodies, positioned in all manner of poses for a baffled audience.

Plastinated bodies are malleable but durable. You could for example, have yourself fashioned into a useful piece of

Mum, you've left Granny too close to the radiator.

furniture or simply displayed for decoration in your family home. It's an eminently more elegant solution for humans than taxidermy.

> 'A friend of mine stopped smoking, drinking, overeating and chasing women – all at the same time. It was a lovely funeral.'
>
> ANONYMOUS

Wheelie-bin burial

If you're one of those people who has joked, 'When I go, just leave me out in the wheelie bin,' then perhaps you should make it part of your funeral surprise. I personally think wheelie-bin coffins are going to be the next big thing. Why not get ahead of the trend?

> 'I am ready to meet my maker. Whether my maker is prepared for the ordeal of meeting me is another matter.'
>
> WINSTON CHURCHILL

LOCATION, LOCATION, LOCATION

Choosing Your Final Resting Place

Compact and economical, perfect for the older lady or gentleman.

So you've scripted your pithy dying words, carved your own hilarious epitaph and stuffed your last will and testament with particularly choice remarks about undeserving relatives. But have you given any thought to what is arguably the most important decision: where to spend the rest of eternity?

Fortunately, there are plenty of places to choose from, but with the most desirable locations filling up quickly, it's worth staking your claim sooner rather than later. Like the mortal property market, location and amenities are key considerations here – but proper research on your potential neighbours is absolutely essential. Wherever you end up, just make sure you're surrounded by your sort of people: you're going to be stuck with them for a very, very long time.

STRIKE A POSE

For deceased posers and exhibitionists, there is no better place to be seen than the fashionable 'ossuary' in Sedlec, Czech Republic, whose daring décor is entirely made up of human skulls and bones. The chapel boasts genuine Gothic charm: built in the early fifteenth century, it was subsequently kitted out with exhumed remains from the adjoining cemetery by a half-blind monk. The current furnishings date from the late nineteenth century, when a local woodcarver renovated the outdated interior design, creating festive skull chains, elaborate coats of arms (and legs, and ribs) and a vast chandelier incorporating every bone in the human body. With over 40,000 residents already in place, Sedlec is a popular but exclusive option for those keen to be seen.

Famous Last Words

'This isn't *Hamlet* you know.
It's not meant to go in my bloody ear!'

A fitting, if disgruntled last utterance from one of the most celebrated Shakespearian actors, LAURENCE OLIVIER (1907–89), when his nurse accidentally spilt water on his face when giving him a drink. He is, of course, referring to the death of Old King Hamlet, who was murdered by his brother pouring poison in his ear as he slept.

LEAVE 'EM LAUGHING

If morbid mourning is the last thing you want – or rather, if it is not the last thing you want – the Merry Cemetery in Sapanta, Romania, could be the final resting place for you. Here scenes from the lives of the dear departed are played out

I TOLD YOU I WAS ILL

across hand-painted headstones in vibrant cartoons and colourful rhymes. The community motto is that death is a celebration of greater things to come. With never a dull moment to be had, it is little wonder that Sapanta has become a popular destination with day trippers and the deceased alike.

> 'Early to rise and early to bed makes a male healthy and wealthy and dead.'
>
> JAMES THURBER, AUTHOR AND WIT

GET AWAY FROM IT ALL

Fans of the quiet life: your search ends here. The isolated islands of Tristan da Cunha (population: 260) are the remotest inhabited place on earth, situated in the middle of the vast expanse of Atlantic Ocean between Africa and South America. If you're a particularly advanced misanthrope, you can do little better than have yourself despatched to Inaccessible Island, part of the archipelago of Tristan da Cunha; although, as its name suggests, the island is sadly lacking in formal burial facilities. Far better to make your peace, quite literally, with Tristan da Cunha's seven native families and their small graveyard on The Settlement, the main island. If you can bag one of the highly sought-after spots on the periphery of the cemetery, beautiful views over the ocean await.

HANG LOOSE

Are you daredevil enough to hang out with the Igorot people of the Philippines? Only the hardiest extreme-sports enthusiasts need apply for a burial spot in remote Echo Valley in Sagada, where coffins are not buried but rather affixed as high up as possible on the sides of sheer limestone cliffs. In a time-honoured tradition going back a few millennia, those who feel the end might be nigh construct their own sturdy coffins, which are then – in due course – winched into place among other members of the community. Remote as they may be, the Igorot are fully aware of the property-scout's motto – 'location, location, location' – and have cornered this hair-raising market for its closer proximity to heaven. Echo Valley's residents-only access has the added benefit of keeping crime stats enviably low.

START YOUR OWN LITERARY SALON

Avid readers will have spent hours on end daydreaming about the vast literary salon that is the afterlife, deciding which cherished authors to dazzle with bons mots and which to deflate with a well-timed riposte. Well, bibliophiles, the world's most intimidating book club does indeed exist, at Highgate Cemetery in London. Once initiated into the inner circle of this exclusive gated community, you can joke with George Eliot, blather with Beryl Bainbridge, rant with the Rosettis and Radclyffe Hall, digress with Douglas Adams and Dickens's nearest and dearest – and even rub shoulders with the great bearded fellow himself, Karl Marx. While the longstanding residents are an agreeable bunch, new arrivals are advised to keep their tortured teenage poems and unpublished novels to themselves.

┌─ **Famous Last Words** ─────────────────┐

'Die, I should say not, dear fellow.
No Barrymore would allow such a
conventional thing to happen to him.'

The last words of JOHN BARRYMORE (1882–1942),
a fast-living eccentric and member of the famous acting
dynasty. Barrymore had four wives and innumerable
mistresses throughout his life and once threw a fish at an
audience member who coughed during his performance.

└───┘

SPY ON THE NEIGHBOURS

If your interest in the great and good is more of the curtain-twitching variety, you need look no further than Père-Lachaise Cemetery in Paris, the best place on earth for picking up and spreading lurid gossip about your neighbours. Frankly, you can give the cold shoulder to your common-or-garden French celebs – Proust, Molière, Balzac, Marcel Marceau – and instead bag a spot within eavesdropping distance of the wealth of controversial characters: Sarah Bernhardt, Maria Callas, Edith Piaf, Isadora Duncan, Héloïse and Abélard, Gertrude Stein and Alice B. Toklas … The absolute crème de la crème at Père-Lachaise, however – and kudos if you can wangle it – is a grave alongside Jim Morrison or Oscar Wilde, whose cult following ensures a gossip-monger's goldmine of passing traffic.

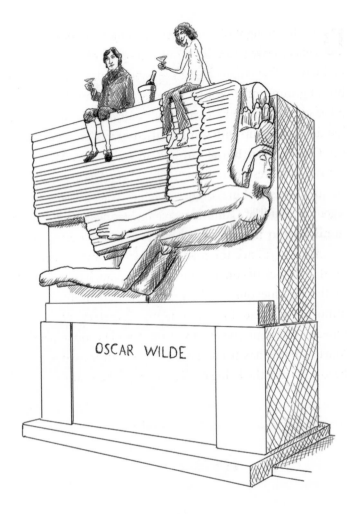

OSCAR WILDE

DO NOT GO QUIETLY

Does the thought of lying back and enjoying the cemetery scenery leave you cold? Would you prefer to be kept busy and have a few laughs along the way? If so, haunting your burial ground may well be the answer. Ghoulish practical jokes can of course be carried out anywhere, but if you're looking to gang up with some kindred spirits, your best bet is the Old Western Burial Ground in Baltimore, Maryland, whose chief resident, Edgar Allen Poe, sets a very high standard in spookiness. The cemetery is also home to the legendary Skull of Cambridge, which belongs to a murdered minister who never stopped screaming, even after death. Attempts to silence the maddening sound by encasing the head in a block of concrete proved futile, much to the delight of the mischievous minister. For an even more macabre atmosphere, head for Saint Louis Cemetery #1 in New Orleans, Louisiana, where notorious Creole voodoo priestess Marie Laveau has been spotted – sometimes without her head – scaring the living daylights out of the visitors.

Famous Last Words

'Why not? After all, it belongs to Him.'

A funny man till the end, CHARLIE CHAPLIN (1889–1977)
responds to the priest at this deathbed asking god to
have mercy on his soul.

'I don't want to achieve immortality
through my work; I want to achieve it
through not dying.'

WOODY ALLEN, WRITER AND DIRECTOR

A GREAT CAREER MOVE

The World's
Ten Top-Earning Dead Celebrities

While newspapers and magazines the world over concern themselves with the wealth and extravagance of kings, sheikhs, oligarchs and other assorted celebrities, *Forbes* magazine must be given due credit for spotting an obvious hole in the market. Each year dozens of celebs drop off the front pages having moved on to the giant after-party in the sky, but their fame keeps the fortune rolling in. And so, with thanks to Forbes and its macabre foresight, I present the ten top-earning dead celebrities (2011 figures).

1. Michael Jackson: $170 million (died 2009)

The King of Pop earned as much criticism as he did praise during his forty-five years in the limelight, but his financial earnings far outstripped both. After very humble beginnings in a small and crowded house in Gary, Indiana, Jackson gradually worked his way up from backing percussionist in The Jackson Five to the most famous performer of the late twentieth century – and immense wealth followed.

During the 1980s in particular he was known for his gold-studded military jackets, crystal-encrusted gloves and even rhinestone-beaded socks. Alongside a vast and eccentrically extravagant wardrobe of costumes, Jackson amassed a gallery's worth of fine art, antiques and other treasures, not to mention his very own amusement park, Neverland, which was valued at $100 million in 2003. He owned the patent for the anti-gravity shoes he wore for his 'Smooth Criminal' music video and also owned the rights to most of The Beatles' songs.

By the time he died in 2009, Jackson was severely in debt and having to sell or auction many of his possessions while also preparing for a lucrative but overly ambitious performance schedule. Nonetheless, his death inevitably sparked renewed commercial interest in all things Jackson, and a combination of music, merchandizing and his posthumous success in the film *This Is It* brought in a small fortune for his estate. *Forbes'* estimate is conservative in comparison to *Billboard*, which calculated that Jackson earned $1 billion in the year following his death.

Famous Last Words

'Why should I talk to you?
I've just been talking to your boss.'

The final words of con-artist, thief and wit
WILSON MIZNER (1876–1933) when he awoke on his
deathbed to find a priest by his side. The criminal
Mizner always conducted himself with humour. He is
reputed to have once held up a sweet shop shouting,
'Your chocolates or your life.'

2. Elvis Presley: $55 million (died 1977)

From the King of Pop to his former father-in-law, the King of rock 'n' roll: Elvis Presley continues to rake in tens of millions of dollars almost forty years after leaving the building for the last time. Before Michael Jackson's untimely demise in 2009, Elvis had spent five consecutive years at the top of the Forbes list. The two of them also shared a passion for outlandish clothing, spectacular showmanship and exuberant living. During his twenty-year career as a much-screamed-after singer and actor, Elvis earned an estimated $4.3 billion, much of which was apparently squandered in his later years. He is rumoured to have died with a mere $5 million in the bank.

The King's home, Graceland, was opened to the public in 1982 and is now second only to the White House on the list of most visited American homes, drawing in over 500,000 fans each year. The dawn of digital downloads has also been good for him: in 2002, a remixed version of 'A Little Less Conversation' became a worldwide number-one hit, while a series of re-releases has made him a regular feature on bestseller lists. Meanwhile, Cirque du Soleil's *Viva Elvis* show in Las Vegas is bringing the King's music to a whole new generation – and a new source of revenue to his estate.

> 'Nothing can be said to be certain,
> except death and taxes.'
>
> BENJAMIN FRANKLIN, 'Founding Father' of America

3. Marilyn Monroe: $27 million (died 1962)

Born Norma Jeane Mortenson on 1 June 1926, Marilyn had a childhood about as far removed from the glamour of Hollywood as is imaginable. With no father on the scene and a mentally ill mother, she spent periods in foster care and an orphanage. But this rags-to-riches starlet eventually hit the big time and, despite only making thirty films in her lifetime, she achieved legend status for her onscreen magic.

Now, fifty years after her death, Monroe is back – co-starring with Charlize Theron in an advert for Dior's J'Adore fragrance. Authentic Brands Group bought the rights to Monroe's estate in 2011 and aim to boost her image further still. The 2012 film *My Week With Marilyn*, starring Michelle Williams as Monroe, will have gone some way to increasing her already huge notoriety. In the pipeline is a chain of Marilyn Monroe cafes.

4. Charles M. Schulz: $25 million (died 2000)

Charles M. Schulz enjoyed middling success as a cartoonist for his local Minneapolis paper in the late 1940s, but when in 1950 he created a thinking, writing, baseball-playing beagle and rooftop aviator named Snoopy, the whole world fell in love with his work. Schulz's comic strip *Peanuts* ran daily in an ever-increasing list of newspapers for fifty years, during which he kept to a strict routine and, unusually, insisted on doing all the colouring and lettering himself. The last original strip appeared on 13 February 2000, the day after his death.

While Schulz is thought to have earned around $1 billion from Charlie Brown and the gang during his lifetime, his posthumous finances have been boosted by continued syndication of repeats of the *Peanuts* strip, alongside merchandizing, books and motion cartoons. The brand was sold for $175 million in 2010, with Charles M. Schulz Creative Associates retaining a healthy 20 per cent stake. Good grief!

5. Elizabeth Taylor: $12 million (died 2011)

One of film's most famous leading ladies, and one of its most beautiful, Taylor starred in over fifty films and won two Academy Awards. She was also devoted to raising money in the fight against AIDS and was the co-founder of the American Foundation for AIDS research (AmFAR). But Liz is perhaps best known for her eight marriages (two of them to the same man, Richard Burton).

One of the last old-school glamorous movie stars, she has a successful perfume, White Diamonds, which is raking it in and, at the end of 2011, Christie's auctioned off her jewels, art and gowns in a sale that fetched over $150 million, setting a world record. No doubt she ought to be higher up this list, but we'll just have to wait and see what her estate's executors decide to do with all that cash.

6. John Lennon: $12 million (died 1980)

The most popular and most eccentric of The Beatles, John Lennon was unsurprisingly a multimillionaire at the time of his murder in December 1980. Despite a turbulent start in life and a fairly disastrous academic record, Lennon put his musical talent to good use by forming The Quarrymen when he was fifteen years old. Six years later, in 1962, the renamed and largely repopulated band was in the grip of 'Beatlemania', a hysterical level of fandom that makes even 'Bieber Fever' look restrained.

Lennon's posthumous popularity was never in doubt, but his bank balance has been particularly healthy over the past few years thanks to a number of tie-ins and endorsements he would quite likely have found bemusing. Alongside a number of digital re-releases to mark what would have been his seventieth birthday in 2010, his hits are played on toy guitars the world over thanks to *The Beatles: Rock Band* video game, while his name and music are used to flog everything from IT solutions to fountain pens. Lennonmania is live and well down here, then, although whether he's 'more popular than Jesus' in the afterlife remains to be seen.

Famous Last Words

'Of course God will forgive me.
That's his job.'

German author, HEINRICH HEINE (1797–1856),
puts a priest in his place with his dying breath.

7. Albert Einstein: $10 million (died 1955)

Given that he is famous for a theory that most people neither understand nor have any practical use for, Albert Einstein makes rather a surprise appearance on the rich list. During his lifetime, he won a Nobel Prize for effectively inventing modern physics and he then set in motion the development of nuclear weapons – two feats for which we are all no doubt grateful. He also published a great many books and articles. But he remained a man of relatively modest means.

Einstein's posthumous wealth has little to do with his discoveries and much to do with his iconic name and appearance. In his will he bequeathed his papers and letters to the Hebrew University of Jerusalem, but most importantly he also bequeathed it any royalties from the use of his name and image. Anything with Einstein stamped on it – from Disney's Baby Einstein range of educational toys to a cartoon of the great man in an advertisement for an Italian bank – is guaranteed to have been approved, at a cost, by the Einstein estate.

8. Dr Seuss: $9 million (died 1991)

No child's bookshelf is complete without a collection of Dr Seuss's eclectic creations, which goes some way to explaining why he is among the bestselling children's authors in history, and why he has a place on this list. Dr Seuss – aka Theodor Seuss Geisel, not a real doctor – published forty-four books in his lifetime, of which the best-loved include *Horton Hatches the Egg, Green Eggs and Ham, The Cat in the Hat* and *How the*

Grinch Stole Christmas. The illustrations in his books are almost as iconic as his catchy rhyme scheme, and all were drawn by the author. He won three Oscars for his short films and documentaries.

Alongside continued sales of his books, Dr Seuss's estate is kept in the black by the Seuss Landing attraction at Florida's Universal Studios theme park and feature films of *Horton Hears a Who* and *How the Grinch Stole Christmas*, both starring Jim Carrey, and *The Cat in the Hat* starring Mike Myers. Dr Seuss has even posthumously lent his name to a number of iPhone apps featuring his eccentric characters.

'There are more dead people than living.
And their numbers are increasing.
The living are getting rarer.'
EUGENE IONESCO, PLAYWRIGHT AND ABSURDIST

9. Jimi Hendrix: $7 million (died 1970)

One of the most experimental electric guitar heroes of all time, Hendrix was only a superstar for the four years leading up to his premature death from an overdose of sleeping pills. He spent the early years of his career backing other artists and lacked confidence in his voice. But his spellbinding playing style and obvious charisma often stole the limelight away from the frontmen. As soon as the Jimi Hendrix Experience was formed in 1966, success came knocking. Today, the icon lives on, with posthumous releases from his estate, including two live show DVDs. Combined with steady catalogue sales and songs like 'Foxy Lady' featuring in global advertising campaigns, the revolutionary figure of rock 'n' roll rocks on.

10. Stieg Larsson: $7 million (died 2004)

For someone who died with absolutely no inkling that he was about to become an international household name, Swedish author Stieg Larsson makes a very impressive entry on our alternative rich list. Writing was a hobby for Larsson and he wrote the three novels in his bestselling Millennium series when he got home from his main job running an anti-far-right foundation. Shortly before he died of a heart attack at the age of fifty, he submitted the trilogy to a Swedish publisher and the rest is very well-documented history.

Sales of *The Girl with the Dragon Tattoo*, *The Girl Who Played with Fire* and *The Girl Who Kicked the Hornets' Nest* continue to soar into the tens of millions, helped along by the highly acclaimed Swedish films of the same names and the more recent American-made equivalents starring Daniel Craig. Larsson is likely to remain on the rich list for years to come: his partner Eva Gabrielsson is in possession of an unfinished fourth Millennium novel and plans to finish it off on his behalf.

Famous Last Words

'Good, a woman who can fart is not dead.'

Thus exclaimed the COMTESSE DE VERCELLIS just after breaking wind, and sadly, just before expiring. Her final act and utterance were recorded for posterity by the philosopher Jean Jacques Rouseau (1712–78) in his autobiographical *Confessions*.

LAUGH?
I NEARLY DIED

Joking About the End

It might not prevent death, but laughter is a pretty good medicine all the same. What better than to laugh at death itself? As these jokes will testify, where there's mortality there's comedy gold.

I live every day like it's my last. Every day I get up at the crack of dawn and spend maybe three hours on the phone making funeral arrangements.

Don and Eddie, two amateur hunters, were out tracking deer in the forest one day. After what felt like an hour sitting uncomfortably in the bushes on one side of a clearing, Don heard a promising cracking of twigs and looked up to see something emerging from the undergrowth on the opposite side.

Able at last to stand up, he leapt into the air, swung his gun towards the creature and pulled the trigger. It let out a pained bellow as it crashed to the ground, followed rather unexpectedly by a string of expletives. Don was filled with horror.

'Oh, God!' he cried as he ran over to his semi-conscious friend. 'Eddie! Oh my God!'

Don pulled out his mobile phone and dialled the emergency services.

'Help me!' he yelled as soon as his call was answered. 'I think I've killed my friend!'

'OK, sir, calm down,' intoned the woman down the line. 'I can help you but you must be calm. First of all, we need to check that your friend is actually dead.'

Silence – and then a shot.

'OK, done,' said Don. 'What next?'

Steve goes on holiday and asks his brother Paul to watch his house. About a week later, Steve calls home to ask how things are going.

'Yup, great,' answers Paul. 'All fine.'

'And my cat?' asks Steve. 'How's he?'

'Oh hell, sorry,' Paul suddenly recalls. 'It's dead.'

'What?!' shrieks Steve. 'I can't believe you just told me like that! You should have worked up to it slowly. The first time I called, you should have told me he was on the roof. The second time I called, you should have said there was no way to get him down. The third time I called, you should have told me that you tried to get him off the roof, but he slipped down and died.'

Paul apologizes and winds up the conversation.

About a week later, Steve calls again.

'No problems at this end,' reports Paul. 'Oh, but I need to tell you about Grandma. She's, erm … Well, she's on the roof.'

Famous Last Words

'Die, my dear doctor?
That is the last thing I shall do!'

An indignant LORD PALMERSTON (1784–1865),
prime minister of Britain, unintentionally points out the
obvious to his doctor before expiring.

Three friends die in a plane crash and find themselves at an orientation session up in heaven.

They are asked to picture their own funerals and imagine what they would like to hear their friends and family saying about them over the coffin.

The first guy says, 'I would like to hear them say that I was a great doctor and a wonderful family man.'

The second guy says, 'I would like to hear that I was a fantastic husband and an inspiring schoolteacher who made a huge difference to the children of tomorrow.'

The last guy thinks for a while before answering.

'I would like to hear them all say, "Oh my God, look! He's moving!"'

Carl: My old man knew the exact date he was going to die. He got the year and the day of the week right and everything. Even the time of day.

Joe: Wow, that's incredible. How on earth did he know all of that?

Carl: A judge told him.

One night, a father overheard his son saying his prayers.

'God bless Mum, Dad and Grandma. Goodbye, Grandpa.'

The father thought this was strange, but soon forgot about it. The next day, the grandfather died.

About a month or so later, the father again overheard his son's prayers.

'God bless Mum and Dad. Goodbye, Grandma.'

The next day, the grandmother died. The father began to worry about his son's morbid powers.

Two weeks later, the father again heard his son praying.

'God bless Mum. Goodbye, Dad.'

This alone nearly gave the father a heart attack, but he survived a sleepless night and went to work the next morning. He stayed in his office all day, waiting for the inevitable. Finally, once it had gone midnight, he went home. He was still alive! He crawled into bed with his wife and apologized.

'I'm sorry, honey, I had a really bad day.'

'You had a bad day?' his wife yelled, sitting up. 'The milkman dropped dead on our doorstep this morning!'

> 'He was a great patriot, a humanitarian,
> a loyal friend – provided, of course,
> that he really is dead.'
> VOLTAIRE, PLAYWRIGHT

An elderly couple were on a cruise and enjoying a romantic evening watching the stars from the deck. Suddenly, a freak storm whipped up and a huge wave washed the old woman overboard. They searched for days and couldn't find her, so the captain sent the old man back to shore with the promise that he would notify him as soon as they found something.

Three weeks went by and the old man finally received a fax from the boat. It read: 'Sir, we are sorry to inform you that we found your wife dead at the bottom of the ocean. We hauled her back up and discovered an oyster attached to her containing a pearl worth about £50,000. Please advise.'

The old man scribbled a hasty reply: 'Send me the pearl and re-bait the trap.'

Three men were standing in line to get into heaven one evening. It had been a pretty hectic day at the pearly gates, however, and it was nearly time for St Peter to call it a day.

'Look,' he told the men, 'I've had a hell of a day and I don't have time to process you all before I knock off. Whichever of you has the best death story can get in tonight.'

'I'll win hands down,' said the first guy. 'For weeks now I've suspected my wife has been cheating on me, so today I came home early to catch her in the act. As I got out of the lift on the twenty-fifth floor, I sensed something was wrong, but my wife wasn't in and I couldn't find anyone else in the apartment. The last place I looked was the balcony, and sure enough I find a naked guy hanging off the railing. Needless to say I was pretty cheesed off, so I started beating and kicking him, but he wouldn't fall. Finally I went back into my apartment and got a hammer and starting hammering on his fingers. Of course, he couldn't stand that for long, so he let go and fell – but even after falling down twenty-five floors he landed in the bushes and survived. I couldn't stand for that, obviously, so I ran into the kitchen, wheeled our refrigerator onto the balcony, and pushed it over the side. I was in luck – it fell on top of him and killed him instantly. Unfortunately, the rage was too much for me and I had a heart attack and died right there.'

'Wow, that sounds a pretty bad day to me,' said St Peter, starting to open the gate.

'Hang on,' said the second man, 'You haven't heard anything yet. I've had the weirdest day. You see, I live on the twenty-sixth floor of this apartment building, and every morning I practise naked yoga out on my balcony. Well, this morning when I was stretching my legs on the railing, I somehow slipped and fell over the edge. Luckily I managed to grab hold of the railing below but I'd only been hanging there for a couple of minutes when this lunatic burst out of the apartment and started attacking me. I was able to hold him off but when he came at me with a hammer I lost my grip and fell to the ground. I was lucky again and landed in the bushes, but no sooner had I got to my feet than – wait for it – a refrigerator came falling out of the sky and crushed me, and now I'm here.'

'I'm impressed!' said St Peter, pushing the gate open again. 'You're in. Unless this last guy can do any better?'

'OK, picture it,' said the third man, coming forward. 'I'm naked, I'm hiding in a refrigerator ...'

Famous Last Words

'My exit is the result of too many entrees.'

The British politician, writer and gourmet ROBERT MONCKTON MILNES (1809–85) took the unusual step of turning his final utterance into a culinary pun.

An old lady is very upset as her beloved Alfie has just passed away. She goes to the funeral home to have one last look at her dearly departed husband, and bursts into tears as soon as she sees him.

One of the undertakers strides up to provide comfort in this sombre moment. Through her tears she explains that she is particularly upset because her darling Alfie is wearing a black suit, when it was his dying wish to be buried in a blue suit.

The undertaker apologizes and explains that, traditionally, bodies are always put in a black suit, but that he'll see what he can arrange.

The next day the old lady returns to the funeral home to have one last moment with Alfie. When the undertaker pulls back the curtain, she manages to smile through her tears. He is resplendent in a smart blue suit.

'Wonderful, just wonderful,' she says to the undertaker. 'But where did you get that lovely blue suit?'

'I think the gods were smiling down upon us, Madam,' he answers. 'After you left yesterday, a man of around your husband's size was brought in and he was wearing a blue suit. His wife explained that she was particularly upset as he'd always wanted to be buried in a black suit, so …'

The wife smiled benignly through her grief.

'… it was really just a simple matter of swapping the heads.'

George is driving along the highway after a stressful day at work, when the car radio suddenly switches from soft rock to an urgent news bulletin.

'Attention all drivers on the highway out of town!' says the newsreader. 'We have just received reports of a car driving in the wrong direction in the fast lane. I repeat: there is a car driving in the wrong direction on the highway.'

'One?' screams George, swerving to avoid yet another oncoming vehicle. 'There are hundreds of them!'

When her husband passed away, Mrs Lamb went to place an obituary in the local paper. The kindly man at the 'Births, Deaths and Marriages' desk commiserated with her about good old George – didn't it always happen to the best ones, etc. – and told her it'd cost a dollar per word. Mrs Lamb thanked him for his generous tribute, grumbled a bit about only having two dollars on her, and then wrote out the best obituary she could afford: 'George died.'

The newsman felt rather bad about this, what with George having been such a great guy, and said he'd throw in three extra words for free. Mrs Lamb was touched. She thanked him profusely and rewrote the obituary: 'George died. Car for sale.'

Two friends, Brian and Bob, were the biggest baseball fans on the planet. They talked about the sport day in and day out, from youth into old age. They shared season tickets and had their names inscribed on their seats at the stadium. They had even vowed that the first to die would come back to tell the other whether or not the great game was played up among the clouds.

One night, having watched his team pull off a resounding victory, Bob passed away in his sleep.

A few nights later, Brian awoke to the sound of Bob's voice from somewhere 'beyond'.

'Bob?' he whispered into the darkness. 'Is that you?'

'Of course it's me!' came the reply. 'Who else?'

'This is unbelievable!' cried Brian. 'So, OK, first things first: is there baseball in heaven?'

'Well, I have some good news and some bad news for you. Which do you want to hear first?'

'Good news first.'

'The good news,' said Bob, 'is that there's baseball in heaven.'

'Wonderful, wonderful!' exclaimed Brian. 'What on earth could be the bad news?'

'You're pitching tomorrow night.'

'Biography lends to death a new terror.'

OSCAR WILDE, PLAYWRIGHT AND WIT

Lying in his hospital bed, a dying man began waving his arms and pointing at his face and generally acting as if he very much wanted to speak. The priest keeping vigil at his bedside leaned over and whispered, 'Do you have something you'd like to say?'

The man nodded and the priest handed him a scrap of paper and a pencil.

'I know you can't speak,' he said quietly, 'but write a note and I'll give it to your wife. She's waiting just outside.'

Gathering his last bit of strength, the man took the paper and scrawled a message, which he stuffed into the priest's hands. Moments later, he died.

Having administered the last rites, the priest left to break the sad news to the man's wife. After consoling her for a few minutes, he handed her the note.

'He had some last words for you,' he explained sympathetically. 'He wrote them down.'

The wife tearfully unfolded the note: 'GET OFF MY OXYGEN PIPE!'

Boss: Do you believe in life after death?

Intern: Yes, sir, I do.

Boss: Aha, well that explains a thing or two. After you left early on Friday to go to your grandmother's funeral, she dropped by to bring you some lunch.

A convicted murderer is about to be executed in the electric chair.

'Do you have a last request?' asks the chaplain.

'Absolutely,' replied the murderer. 'Will you hold my hand?'

Celia, a woman on the wrong side of middle age, suffers a heart attack while eating a hamburger and is rushed to hospital. While on the operating table she has a near-death experience and sees God standing before her in a warm glow of light.

'Is this it?' she asks him, panicked.

'No, no, no,' God reassures her. 'You have another twenty-eight years to go.'

This fixes Celia's resolve: today is the first day of the rest of her life. As soon as she's discharged from hospital she readmits herself for a vigorous round of collagen shots, cheek implants, liposuction and breast augmentation. She even gets one of the nurses to dye her hair.

Feeling as fantastic as she looks, she marches out of the hospital and is struck down and killed by a speeding ambulance.

'Hello?!' she yells when she is brought before God. 'What the hell happened to my twenty-eight years?'

'Celia?' God exclaims. 'I'm so sorry – I didn't recognize you!'

A lifelong Republican is lying on his deathbed when he suddenly announces he wants to join the Democrats.

'Why on earth would you want to do that?' asks his puzzled wife. 'You're Republican through and through. Why change now?'

The man leans forward.

'I'd rather it was one of them that died and not one of us.'

Famous Last Words

'Martha, hand me my pantaloons
if you please.'

American poet FITZ-GREENE HALLECK (1790–1867)
presumably hoped to die with a little dignity.
Hard when you're wearing pantaloons. And your parents
called you 'Fitz-Greene'.

A man went up to the counter at his local library and said to the woman there, 'Have you got any books about committing suicide?'

The librarian gave him a helpful smile and said, 'Of course, sir. Just to the left over there – on the middle shelf.'

The man wandered over but came back almost immediately.

'I'm sorry,' he said, 'but the shelf you said seems to be empty. I can't find any at all.'

The librarian sighed.

'It's a bit of a nightmare, actually,' she confessed. 'They never bring them back.'

A condemned man asked the sheriff, 'Say, are you really going to make me die swinging from a tree?'

'No, of course not!' replied the sheriff.

The man breathed a sigh of relief.

'All we do,' said the sheriff, 'is put a rope around your neck and kick the horse away. After that it's up to you.'

John: Hey Peter, I was so sorry to hear you buried your mother last week.

Peter: Oh, well, thanks. But, you know, we had to. She was dead.

A man dies and finds himself at the gates of heaven. God is standing there with a large book.

'Well, Steve,' says God, 'I have looked you up in the *Book of Life* and you sound a pretty decent guy. You can come in under one condition.'

'OK, what is it?'

'You must spell the word "love",' God answers.

Steve spells the word correctly and God disappears in a flash of light and a chorus of angels. The gate swings open.

He starts walking tentatively towards what seems to be the recreation area, but suddenly he hears the shrill voice of his wife back at the gate.

'Steve!' she shrieks. 'Come here right now and let me in!'

'What are you doing here?' he asks.

'Well, I'm dead,' she snorts. 'Some moron ran into me on my way home from your do – sorry, funeral – and here I am. Now quit talking and let me in.'

'Alright,' says Steve. 'But before you enter heaven there's this one word you have to spell.'

'And that word is … ?'

'Floccinaucinihilipilification.'

A priest was midway through his usual dreary sermon when a freak storm hit and the church was battered by torrential rain. Members of the congregation began to leave, politely at first but with a mounting sense of panic once the church began to flood. The priest declined to join them.

'God will save me,' he said.

Two hours later, with the water up around his waist, the priest was still refusing to budge. A man paddled into the church on a raft and told the priest to hop aboard, but it was hopeless.

'God will save me,' he said.

By late afternoon, he had been forced up onto the roof of the church. A police crew pulled up alongside in a boat and the chief urged him to climb in.

'God will save me,' was all the priest would say.

When it became dark and all the boats had sailed away, a military helicopter hovered into view. Its searchlight trained on the drenched priest, the helicopter captain let down a rope ladder and commanded him to grab hold of it.

'No, thank you!' shouted the priest. 'God will save me!'

An hour later the priest found himself at the gates of heaven. God was there, looking annoyed.

'God!' exclaimed the priest. 'Why didn't you save me from that terrible flood?'

'I sent you a raft, a boat and a helicopter!' yelled God. 'What more could you possibly want from me?'

Paul is on his deathbed with his best friend and business partner Jack at his side.

'Jack, I've got to confess,' says Paul, 'I've been sleeping with your wife for the past thirty years, your daughter is in fact my daughter, and I've been stealing from our firm for a decade.'

'Relax,' says Jack, 'and don't think another thing about it. I'm the one who put arsenic in your martini.'

A woman visits a fortune-teller who tells her: 'Prepare yourself to be a widow. Your husband will die a violent and horrible death this year.'

Visibly shaken, the woman takes a few deep breaths, steadies her voice and asks: 'Will I be acquitted?'

Phoning the florist to order some flowers for her lover's funeral, Jean was caught off guard when asked what message she wanted on the card.

'Message?' she sputtered. 'Well, I guess: "You will be missed".'

Come the day of the funeral, she was delighted that her floral tribute had pride of place but mortified at the message pinned prominently on it: 'Well, I guess you will be missed.'

'When Mozart was my age,
he had been dead for two years.'
TOM LEHRER, PIANIST

LAUGHING IN THE FACE OF UNDEATH

The Pros and Cons of Preternatural Life

If life's a bit drab and the prospect of your inevitable death is a bore, you might like to consider 'undeath' as a pleasing middle ground. Let's face it, it looks a lot more fun then plain old deadness. And heaven too for that matter. You don't have to be nice to long-expired relatives all day long while listening to the heavenly choir sing on and on, strumming their interminable harps. On the contrary – undeath promises fun, adventures, new friends and possibly even a bit of old-style glamour.

ZOMBIES JUST WANNA HAVE FUN (AND EAT BRAINS)

Zombies have come a long way. From the spooky, hypnotized semi-corpses of Haiti's voodoo tradition, through the shambling, groaning, brain-obsessed first zombies of popular culture, to the high-speed killing machines of recent 'zombie apocalypse' films. But there's no doubt that in any or all of these guises being a zombie doesn't seem that bad. They're usually in good company with lots of new zombie friends and 'life' is just so much simpler and freer than in their old workaday world.

It all began in West Africa a few hundred years ago, where adherents to 'Vodou' (voodoo) believed sorcerers (bokors) had the power to revive the dead. This reanimated 'zombie' would essentially have no mind of its own and remain under the sorcerer's control. There was no brain eating in those days, and an easy remedy for getting any stray zombie to return to the grave was to feed it salt. In some South African communities to this day, it is believed that a dead person can be turned into a zombie by certain children – and that only a 'sangoma' or herbal medicine practitioner can return them to the grave.

These days in the Western world, the zombie's transformation from a live person to an undead cannibal is usually attributed to a rogue virus, radiation or some other nebulous cause, expressing a distrust of modern science. The film that kickstarted the zombie genre in cinema was George A. Romero's *The Night of the Living Dead* (1968). In this film we find the mysteriously zombified undead attacking a group of seven people trapped in an isolated farmhouse in Pennsylvania, determined to eat them. While this film was presented as deadly serious, subsequent zombie films have celebrated the madness, chaos and viscera the genre provides for – allowing everyone, ghouls and their prey, to have fun.

Romero followed up *The Night of the Living Dead* with the eminently more light-hearted and gory *Dawn of the Dead* (1978) and *Day of the Dead* (1985). The first finds our heroes barricaded into a shopping mall – which is like catnip to the zombies, who can't resist its bright lights, escalators and chintzy music.

The real fun started however, with Sam Raimi's Evil Dead series in the early 1980s. In the first film teens planning a wild weekend in a cabin in the woods fall prey to an ancient curse and one by one are transformed into bloodthirsty and very persistent zombies who clearly relish their new purpose.

Probably the best advertisement for life as a zombie is Peter 'Lord of the Rings' Jackson's 1992 film, *Braindead*. In this film, a bite from the vicious 'Sumatran Rat-Monkey' at the local zoo turns upstanding mother-of-one Mrs Cosgrove into a delightfully deranged zombie. Her under-the-thumb son Lionel does his best to keep her hidden from the world, but it's only a matter of time before she gets her teeth into some innocent bystanders and soon zombies are cropping up everywhere, despite Lionel's best efforts to keep them contained and sedated in his basement.

Of course, the iconic John Landis-directed music video to Michael Jackson's 'Thriller' shows that zombies really do have all the fun (and the best moves) in a wonderfully choreographed dance of the risen dead led by Mr Jackson in full zombie make-up.

More recently films like *28 Days Later*, *28 Weeks Later* and *I Am Legend* have started taking themselves seriously again with terrifying, high-speed zombies – who nonetheless are still visibly enjoying their new, thoroughly evil undead lives.

The zombie genre has spawned some very special film titles including: *Dead & Breakfast* (2004), *Boy Eats Girl* (2005), *Kung Fu Zombie* (1982), *I Was a Teenage Zombie* (1987), and low budget, horror-comedy musical, *Nudist Colony of the Dead* (1991).

> 'The idea is to die young
> as late as possible.'
> ASHLEY MONTAGU, ANTHROPOLOGIST

VAMPIRES:
THE NEW BLACK

Enjoying something of a revival these days, nobody makes death look more attractive than the vampire. Whether depicted as the brooding emo vampire of Stephenie Meyer's Twilight novels, the buff biters of *Buffy the Vampire Slayer*, the decadent dandies of Anne Rice's *Interview with a Vampire*, or the sinister master of them all, *Dracula*, the vampire has the broadest appeal of all our mythological not-quite-dead creatures.

With their impossible-to-place European accents, languid grace, easy sexuality and penchant for gothic mansions with sensuous velvet-draped interiors – who wouldn't want to be bitten! They always get the best lines, too.

The vampire myth has been around for a very long time, with some scholars suggesting it could have its origins in prehistory. Vampires crop up in the cultures of the ancient Mesopotamians, Hebrews, Greeks and Romans. But the word 'vampire' itself is pretty new and was only popularized in the eighteenth century, when superstitions from the Balkans and Eastern Europe started making their way westward.

It was in John Polidori's 1819 novella *The Vampyre* that the smooth, charismatic vampire was born, to then be perfected in Bram Stoker's *Dracula* (1897). The latter novel pretty much sets the rules for all vampire characters to follow (fear of garlic, crucifixes and the sun, etc.) and is single-handedly responsible for our modern fixation.

Some people take vampires very seriously indeed. In London in the 1970s for example, the atmospheric Highgate Cemetery (page 148) became the alleged haunt of a vampire, attracting droves of amateur vampire hunters there in pursuit. Many in Europe and the US have adopted vampire lifestyles in their bid to join the ranks of the suave undead. Though one needs to be very down with sub-cultures to tell the difference between these new wave 'vampires' and Goths. Either way, keep your jugular covered.

Famous Last Words

'Only one man ever understood me.
And even he didn't understand me.'

The ponderous exhortation upon expiration of philosopher
GEORG WILHELM HEGEL (1770–1831).

'You know what they say:
'You don't have to swim faster than the shark, you just have to swim faster than the person you're with.'
KEVIN NEALON, COMEDIAN

THE MUMMIES' CURSE

Perhaps not the most attractive undead lifestyle option, in popular culture the 'mummy' is the reanimated corpse of a long-buried Egyptian aristocrat or royal. Unlike zombies they don't tend to have much company; like vampires, theirs is a dark sort of existence – but with none of the glamour.

The trajectory of the mummy story usually involves an explorer in khakis breaking into a long-hidden tomb in search of buried riches but unleashing a terrible curse instead. The mummy is a bandage-swathed killing machine and has no precedent in mythology. Instead it is purely an invention of books and later the cinema.

The arrival of this accursed corpse in popular culture coincided with expeditions from Western countries to pillage the tombs of the ancient kings and queens of Egypt in the early nineteenth century. Given the sacrilegious and even dangerous nature of this activity, it lends itself well to creepy tales of ancient curses and revenge.

'A friend of mine just died.
He was eighty-four years old and died
broke. At the funeral, everyone said,
"What a shame, he died penniless."
I don't know – to me that sounds like perfect
timing on a hell of a budget.'

AL CLETHEN, JR, COMEDIAN

Famous Last Words

'I'd rather be skiing.'

ARTHUR STANLEY JEFFERSON (1890–1965), the
'Laurel' half of comedy duo Laurel and Hardy on his
deathbed. He didn't ski.